Jan Latta

Ziggy th ZEBR

Come on a great adventure with me and learn all about my family

TRUE TO LIFE BOOKS

Educating children about endangered animals.

Jan Latta author and wildlife photographer.

Hello. My name is Ziggy and I'm a Burchell zebra.
I live on the grassy plains of Africa with my family.

We first appeared on Earth
about 3 million years ago.

Our cousins are called the Grévy zebra.

Can you see the difference?

We live together in a family group called a **herd**. My father is called a stallion and my mother is called a mare.

When I am young I have tan stripes. They will turn black when I am older.

I drink my mother's rich milk for a year
and I stay with her for up to 3 years.

She is a very special mother
and I love to play and nuzzle up to her.

We are **herbivores** which means we eat grass.
We use our strong teeth for grinding
and cropping grass.

We spend most of the day grazing.
Our home range is always close to water
because we need to drink each day.

Once a year we **migrate** up to 800 kilometres with wildebeest and antelope to search for new grass on the Serengeti plains.

The dominant mare always leads the family group, and the other zebras follow in single file.

Our stripes are like your fingerprints and
every zebra has a different pattern.

The stripes are called disruptive colouration
and they help to break up the outline of our bodies.
This helps to **camouflage** and protect
us from predators. Isn't that clever?

We like to have a **dust bath** by rolling in the dirt.

This helps to clean our skin and protect us from insects.

We have fun **galloping** along the plains and wrestling each other.

Sometimes we like to have a friendly fight
to see who is the strongest male.

We have excellent eyesight, a good sense of smell and we can rotate our ears to locate sounds.

We have single-toed hooves, the same as a horse so we can run and gallop.

ZEBRA FACTS

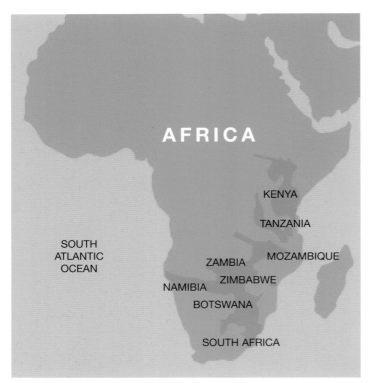

Some of the areas where zebras can be found.

SCIENTIFIC NAME
There are three species of zebras.
Burchell zebra. *Equus Burchelli*
Grévy zebra. *Equus Grevyi*
Mountain zebra. There are two subspecies of mountain zebra.
Equus zebra zebra is endangered
Equus zebra hartmannae is threatened.

HABITAT
Burchell zebras live in a family group on the grasslands and open woodlands in Africa. They stay close to a waterhole as they need to drink every day.
Grévy zebras live in northern Kenya and Ethiopia. Thousands migrate once a year to the Serengeti plains to eat fresh new grass.
Mountain zebras live in Namibia and South Africa in mountainous and hilly habitats. They are a threatened species.

DIET
All zebras eat grass, shrubs, twigs and leaves. They spend 60% of the day grazing. Zebras need to drink water each day. However, the Grévy zebras can survive for up to 5 days without water.

WEIGHT
Zebras weigh from 175 to 387 kilograms. Males weigh 10% more than females.

HEIGHT
Zebras can stand from 1 to 1.47 metres high at the shoulder. They are 2 to 2.5 metres long.

BIRTH
Gestation period is 12 months for the Burchell zebra and 13 months for the Grévy zebra. When a foal is born the mother keeps it away from the herd for 2 or 3 days. Then the foal will recognise its mother by sight, sound and smell.

The Grévy zebra has fine black stripes that fade at their stomach.

The Burchell zebra has wider strips that continue under their stomach.

PREDATORS

Lions and hyenas attack zebras. Also leopards, cheetahs and hunting dogs. If the herd is attacked, they form a semi-circle and kick and bite their predators. Humans are their greatest risk and kill zebras for their meat and skins.

LIFESPAN

Zebras can live 20 to 30 years in the wild and about 40 years in captivity.

NUMBERS REMAINING

Grévy zebras are the most endangered of the 3 species of zebras with fewer that 2,500 remaining in the wild.
Mountain zebras have 2,700 in the wild due to conservation efforts.
Burchell zebras are plentiful on the plains but their numbers are diminishing.

DID YOU KNOW?

- Rare albino zebras have been seen in the Mount Kenya forest in Africa.
- The zebra is a symbol of beauty in the African culture.
- Zebras sleep standing up.
- Zebras have never been domesticated.
- The Grévy zebra is named after Jules Grévy, the president of France in the 1880s, who received a zebra as a gift.
- The Burchell zebra is named after the British explorer, William John Burchell, in southern Africa in 1815.
- Scientists identify zebras by comparing their individual patterns, stripe widths and colour.
- Zebras can gallop up to 56kph. They have great stamina and sometimes they can outrun their predators.
- Zebras travel with wildebeest and antelope during the yearly migration.

CREATING ZIGGY THE ZEBRA BOOK

" To create the zebra book, I travelled to Africa nine times. I lived in a small tent in the Maasi Mara and every day I photographed and wrote about the zebras.

Then I went to the mountains of Samburu, where I saw a spectacular fight between two Grévy zebras who were fighting to be the dominant stallion. The fight lasted 15 minutes with loud braying, barking and snorting sounds. Finally they calmed down, and with their tails in the air, they galloped away.

Grévy zebras fighting for dominance.

Later I travelled to Nanyuki where a herd of Burchell zebras were spooked and they came thundering past my jeep. I was covered in dust and mud and only managed to take a photograph of their striped bottoms disappearing across the grassy plains.

It was interesting to see the difference between the Burchell, Grévy and Mountain zebras. I had to check the shape of their ears and the different pattern of their stripes. "

Jan Latta, author and wildlife photographer.

QUESTIONS

1. Where do zebras live?
2. Name the three different zebras.
3. What makes them different?
4. What do zebras eat?
5. Are zebras related to the horse?
6. How do zebras sleep?
7. What is a burrito sound?
8. When is the zebra migration?
9. Are zebras endangered?
10. What is a herbivore?

FIND THE ZEBRA IN THE GRASS

Colour the shapes with a grey star in green and colour the shapes with a black dot in black.

ZIPPY ZEBRAS

Make a zebra face with a cone of white paper, then paint on the black stripes, eyes, black nose and stick-on ears. Attach to a long stick, add strips of black paper for the zebra's mane and gallop around making zebra noises.

KOALA PORTRAIT

Make a koala face using a white paper plate. Paint the plate grey. Cut out ears, nose and eyes and glue them on. Pick gum branches and leaves and hang them in your class-room so your koalas can live in the trees.

GUMLEAF PRINT

Collect gum leaves and make a paper rubbing of the leaves. Place a flattened leaf under a piece of paper and gently rub a crayon over the top, making sure you don't move the paper.

ORANGUTAN ORANGES

Make an orangutan face on an orange. Place each orange on a flat surface. If it's wobbly ask the teacher to cut a base. Stick on sultanas for eyes and nose and draw on a smile. Use strips of orange paper for its long hair.

GIRAFFE DOT PAINTING

Draw the outline of a giraffe on paper. Use a paintbrush to make an Aboriginal-style dot painting with brown, orange and yellow paints for its coat. Draw on a face, then hooves and a mane.

MEERKAT FINGER PUPPETS

Place two pieces of paper flat in front of you and put your forefinger on top. Draw around the outline of your finger and cut out the shape allowing at least a centimetre extra space. Staple the top and sides together keeping the bottom edges open. Draw the face, arms, legs and add a tail.

RHINO HORN RATTLE

Make a rhino horn with black paper. Take an A4 size piece of paper length-ways and fold the two top corners to the middle and keep folding until you get a horn shape. Tape the horn shape and fill with dried beans. Fold up the bottom edges to seal and tape across.

ELEPHANT MASK

From one side of a cereal box cut out the shape of an elephant's head. Paint it grey or brown. Cut out tusks and ears and glue them on. Make a hole at either side and loop with string or elastic to wear.

PANDA PUPPET

Turn a plain paper bag upside-down to wear as a panda puppet over your hand. Decorate the bag to look like a panda. Draw on a face and then cut out ears and paws and glue them on.

PANDA PLAYTIME

Make a panda face using a paper plate. Paint the face. Cut out ears, nose and eyes and glue them on. Pick bamboo branches. Or pick thin branches and make leaves with green paper, so you can pretend to be a panda in a bamboo forest.

ANIMAL ANCESTORS

Research and list the names of animals that were alive during the Ice Age. A woolly ancestor of the elephant roamed the earth. What was its name? Draw its picture. Why did it become extinct?

CHIMP CHOPSTICKS

Head outdoors, crouch down and use wooden chopsticks to forage for food in the ground. Record what you see at chimp level.

HAPPY LION FACE

Draw a lion's face on paper and paint it yellow. Mark eyes, nose and mouth in black. Glue on ears and stick pasta spirals around the head for a mane.

PAPER PAWS

Draw the shape of a leopard's paw on two paper bags and paint them yellow. Add black leopard spots and claws with a black marker. Wear your fierce leopard paws!

TRACK A TIGER

What are pug marks? Make a set of pug marks with a potato print. Cut a potato in half. Cut out the shape of the pug marks. Dip in paint and make a print of the tiger tracks on paper.

Draw a **LEOPON** a cross between a female lioness and a male leopard. Have lots of fun with your imagination.

CHEETAH WORD GAME

How many words can you make out of the word cheetah? You should be able to make at least five words. Look at the letters and try putting them in different sequences to find new words.

ANIMAL MAP ZONE

On a map of the world find the countries where the animals in the True to Life books live in the wild. Label them with pictures of the animals and the animals' habitats. For example, rainforest, jungle, bamboo forest, savannah, etc.

COLLECTIVE QUIZ

Some groups of animals are described using collective nouns. Here are some from the True to Life books:
A journey of giraffes
A herd of elephants
A pod of hippos
A pride of lions
A crash of rhinos
A leap of leopards
A swift of tigers
A clan of hyenas
A litter of cubs
How many collective nouns can you add?

ANIMAL SUPERSTARS

Look for TV advertisements featuring wild animals and explain why you think that animal has been used for the ad.

DIARY OF A SAFARI

Plan a safari in Kenya.
What animals might you see?
Where will you stop to camp?
Do you live in a tent?
Describe your guide.
What dangers might you face?
Will you see animals hunting?
How will you travel between camps?
What foods will you eat?
Will you be frightened at night?

ENDANGERED ANIMALS

Name some of the most endangered animals in the world. What can you do to help save them from extinction? Name some of the charities that help endangered animals.

ZEBRA POEM *See if you can fill in the missing letters.*

My Dad is a stallion and my Mum is a mare;
I am a foal and we all have black and white h - - -.

I walk, trot and gallop just like a horse;
But I am different because of my s - - - - - - of course.

When I am with my friends we are called a herd all together;
We like to drink water and eat g - - - - when we gather.

colour in the zebra

INTERESTING WEBSITES

KIDS' PLANET
www.kidsplanet.org

SCIENCE KIDS - Fun science & technology for kids
www.science kids.co.nz

NATIONAL GEOGRAPHIC KIDS
www.nationalgeographic.com

WIKIPEDIA
www.wikipedia.org/plains_zebra

AFRICAN WILDLIFE FOUNDATION
www.awf.org/wildlife-conservation/zebra

LIVE SCIENCE
www.livescience.com/27443-zebras

ANIMAL ENCYCLOPEDIA
animals.about.com/od/hoofedmammals/a/tenthingszebras.

AMAZING FACTS ABOUT ZEBRAS
www.onekind.org.be
www.outtoafrica.nl/animals/engzebra
www.ask.com/Zebra+Pictures+And+Facts

Exciting videos of wild animals from the True to Life Books http://bit.ly/13gVVoY

Photography:
Dr. Herbert R. Axelrod, 62; Tom Caravaglia, 40 (bottom); Kent Freeman, 60; Ron Reagan 52 (bottom), 55; Vince Serbin, 44, 46, 47, 48, 51 (bottom), 52 (top); Sally Anne Thompson, 6, 7, 50, 68, 70, 71, 72, 73, 74, 75, 76, 77, 80, 81, 82, 83, 86, 87, 88, 89, 90; Three Lions, Inc., 91

Front Cover:
Poodles are bred in three sizes: Toy, Miniature, and Standard. Their popularity through the years can be attributed to their keen intelligence, their ability to learn, and their marvelous temperament.

Back Cover:
Above: Basset Hounds are wonderful family pets. Shown is a dam with her litter of pups. *Below:* The German Shepherd Dog serves his master both as a companion and a protector. His alert expression, noble stance, and fearlessness command respect from all.

Endpapers:
These English Springer Spaniels make good hunting dogs. Their name derives from their ability to "spring" game.

Frontis:
A pair of King Charles Spaniels.

0-87666-816-3

© 1982 by TFH Publications, Inc. Ltd.

Distributed in the U.S. by T.F.H. Publications, Inc., 211 West Sylvania Avenue, PO Box 427, Neptune, NJ 07753; in England by T.F.H. (Gt. Britain) Ltd., 13 Nutley Lane, Reigate, Surrey; in Canada to the pet trade by Rolf C. Hagen Ltd., 3225 Sartelon Street, Montreal 382, Quebec; in Canada to the book trade by H & L Pet Supplies, Inc., 27 Kingston Crescent, Kitchener, Ontario N28 2T6; in Southeast Asia by Y.W. Ong, 9 Lorong 36 Geylang, Singapore 14; in Australia and the South Pacific by Pet Imports Pty. Ltd., P.O. Box 149, Brookvale 2100, N.S.W. Australia; in South Africa by Valid Agencies, P.O. Box 51901, Randburg 2125 South Africa. Published by T.F.H. Publications, Inc., Ltd.

CONTENTS

The T.F.H. Book of PUPPIES

DR. HERBERT RICHARDS

**with a special section on first aid
by Dr. George D. Whitney, D.V.M.**

Canine loyalty and devotion come in a variety of colors and sizes. Affection, courage, and service exemplify the dog, but above all the dog is a canine companion. Known as "man's best friend," this domesticated animal offers compassion, perception, and intelligence, as well as instinctive talents. Whether a dog is pure-bred or mixed, the dog is a member of the family of canines and of society in general.

Introduction

One of the first animals that man was able to domesticate was the dog. In ancient history, cave men were so attached to their dog companions that they often were found buried with their pets. In more than one civilization (Eskimos and Laplanders), the life of the community was dependent upon the ability of dogs to hunt, protect, herd animals and pull heavy loads over ice and snow.

As our civilization progressed, more and more varieties of dogs have come to light. The long-legged, fast-running Afghan Hound from Afghanistan has been in use for 5,000 years by the nomads of the desert to run down gazelles. The Pekingese has been an old lap dog of the ancient Chinese, who for thousands of years considered it to be a holy animal and restricted their ownership to royalty alone. The Poodle has a long and glorious history as a companion, hunter and swimmer. Terriers were used in Europe for killing rats, and Spaniels were used for hundreds of years for hunting and flushing small animals and birds. Is it any wonder then that there are now over 150 million domesticated dogs in the world?

SPORTING DOGS

AMERICAN WATER SPANIEL

BRITTANY SPANIEL

CHESAPEAKE BAY RETRIEVER

CLUMBER SPANIEL

AMERICAN COCKER SPANIEL

ENGLISH SETTER

Dogs are grouped generally according to their function. The group of Sporting Dogs includes: CHESAPEAKE BAY RETRIEVER, average weight 70 pounds, height about 24 inches, a remarkable dog in the water; AMERICAN COCKER SPANIEL, average weight 25 pounds, height 14 inches, the smallest member of the Sporting Group; AMERICAN WATER SPANIEL, average weight 40 pounds, height 17 inches, possesses a curly coat in the shade of liver or brown; CLUMBER SPANIEL, average weight 55 pounds, height 17 inches, a splendid retriever when trained; ENGLISH SETTER, average weight 65 pounds, height 25 inches, highly favored by sportsmen; BRITTANY SPANIEL, average weight 35 pounds, height 19 inches, hails from France; ENGLISH COCKER SPANIEL, average weight 32 pounds, height 16 inches, an active and merry dog who really enjoys hunting; CURLY-COATED RETRIEVER, average weight 70 pounds, height 23 inches, has dense curly hair; ENGLISH SPRINGER SPANIEL, average weight 50 pounds, height 19 inches, "springs" game from cover when hunting.

Kinds of Dogs

ENGLISH COCKER SPANIEL

CURLY-COATED RETRIEVER

ENGLISH SPRINGER

You have to make a decision about either what kind of dog to select to suit your needs or how to best handle the dog that you now have. The recognized breeds of dogs are broken down into six general groups: Sporting, Hound, Working, Terrier, Toy and Non-sporting, and only a few of the breeds in each group are mentioned here.

The *Sporting Group* of dogs is that group whose primary purpose is to hunt game and large animals and to retrieve game that is killed by their master. Among this group are the pointers, which have the ability to track down game and to freeze to a "point" when they have located the prey. Retrievers, such as the Golden and Labrador, are dogs with great hunting and swimming abilities. Also included in this group are the spaniels and the setters.

In the *Hound Group*, that group of dogs which is supposed to have the keenest scent, tracking ability and the patience to follow and track for hours at a time, are such typical members as the Greyhound, Whippet, Bloodhound, Beagle, Dachshund, the elegant Afghan Hound, and the tallest of all the breeds, the Irish Wolfhound.

Dogs that have been bred to perform such functions as guarding homes, pulling sleds, herding cattle or saving lives are classified within the *Working Group*. Representatives of the group are the Boxer, Great Dane, German Shepherd Dog, Mastiff, Doberman Pinscher, St. Bernard, Newfoundland, Collie, and Rottweiler. All are sturdy dogs that have great stamina and strength of character.

The *Terriers*, which are fine hunting companions since they follow their game right into the ground, come in a variety of sizes. This group is comprised of the Bull Terrier (both white and colored), Irish Terrier, Scottish Terrier, Skye Terrier, West Highland White Terrier, and Miniature Schnauzer, to name a few.

The Toy Poodle, Chihuahua, Pekingese, Pug, and Maltese are among those breeds that belong to the *Toy Group*. Some are merely miniatures of other breeds, and when posed on their owner's lap, they offer much pleasure and companionship.

The *Non-sporting Group*, whose members are as diverse in their backgrounds as they are in their physical appearance, includes the Lhasa Apso, Shih Tzu, Chow Chow, Keeshond, Dalmatian, and both the Miniature and Standard Poodle.

SPORTING DOGS

GERMAN WIRE-HAIRED POINTER

FLAT-COATED RETRIEVER

GORDON SETTER

GERMAN SHORT-HAIRED POINTER

Spaniels flush their game, and Retrievers fetch or retrieve game on land or in water. More examples of dogs in the Sporting Group: GERMAN WIREHAIRED POINTER, average weight 60 pounds, height 24 inches, an aloof and energetic canine with a weather-resisting coat; GORDON SETTER, average weight 65 pounds, height 26 inches, an aristocratic shooting companion with keen intelligence; FLAT-COATED RETRIEVER, average weight 65 pounds, height 23 inches, has great perseverance when hunting and retains a youthful outlook on life; GERMAN SHORTHAIRED POINTER, average weight 65 pounds, height 24 inches, a versatile field-dog with webbed feet and water-repellent coat.

GOLDEN RETRIEVER

POINTER

FIELD SPANIEL

LABRADOR RETRIEVER

IRISH SETTER

WELSH SPRINGER SPANIEL

POINTER, average weight 65 pounds, height 25 inches, a dignified dog of even temperament and good sense; LABRADOR RETRIEVER, average weight 70 pounds, height 23 inches, a strong swimmer with short, dense coat; WELSH SPRINGER SPANIEL, average weight 37 pounds, height 17 inches, a gun dog that is a good guard yet gentle with children and other animals; FIELD SPANIEL, average weight 40 pounds, height 18 inches, a well-balanced dog built for activity and endurance; IRISH SET-TER, average weight 65 pounds, height 25 inches, a bird dog that is bold yet gentle, lovable, and loyal. GOLDEN RETRIEVER, average weight 70 pounds, height 23 inches, a companion dog that is adept in the field, in obedience, and as a guide for the blind.

SPORTING DOGS

IRISH WATER SPANIEL

WIRE-HAIRED POINTING GRIFFON

SUSSEX SPANIEL

VIZSLA

WEIMARANER

More dogs in the Sporting Group: WIRE-HAIRED POINTING GRIF-FON, average weight 60 pounds, height 22 inches, strong and vigorous dog with harsh coat; SUSSEX SPANIEL, average weight 40 pounds, height 15 inches, a determined hunter with a rich golden liver color; WEIMARANER, average weight 75 pounds, height 26 inches, a graceful and alert worker with great speed and endurance in the field; IRISH WATER SPANIEL, average weight 60 pounds, height 24 inches, a grand water dog and an excellent duck retriever; VIZSLA, average weight 65 pounds, height 23 inches, multi-purpose Hungarian Pointer with aristocratic bearing and rusty-gold coat.

HOUNDS

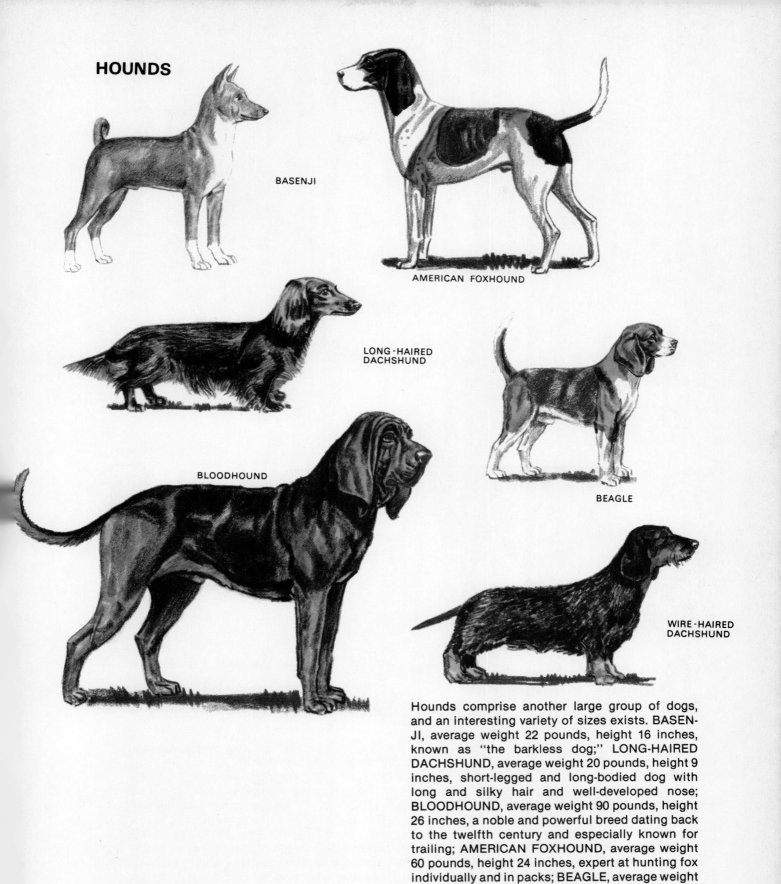

BASENJI

AMERICAN FOXHOUND

LONG-HAIRED DACHSHUND

BLOODHOUND

BEAGLE

WIRE-HAIRED DACHSHUND

Hounds comprise another large group of dogs, and an interesting variety of sizes exists. BASENJI, average weight 22 pounds, height 16 inches, known as "the barkless dog;" LONG-HAIRED DACHSHUND, average weight 20 pounds, height 9 inches, short-legged and long-bodied dog with long and silky hair and well-developed nose; BLOODHOUND, average weight 90 pounds, height 26 inches, a noble and powerful breed dating back to the twelfth century and especially known for trailing; AMERICAN FOXHOUND, average weight 60 pounds, height 24 inches, expert at hunting fox individually and in packs; BEAGLE, average weight 18 pounds for those under 13 inches and 30 pounds for those 13 to 15 inches, excellent for hunting rabbits; WIRE-HAIRED DACHSHUND, average weight 20 pounds, height 9 inches, wiry coat protects against brambles when hunting badgers.

HOUNDS

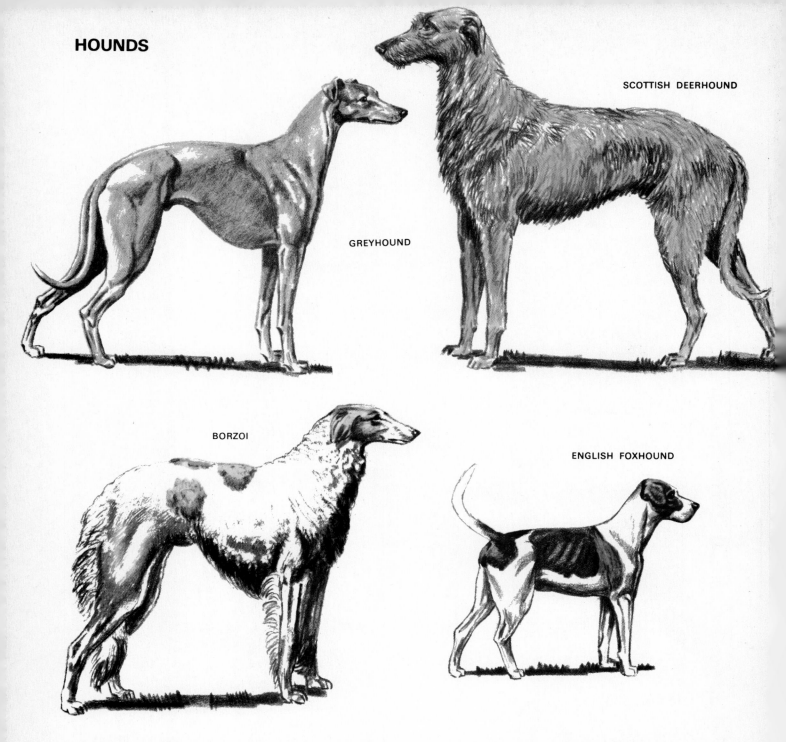

SCOTTISH DEERHOUND

GREYHOUND

BORZOI

ENGLISH FOXHOUND

GREYHOUND, average weight 65 pounds, height 26 inches, swift, graceful, and wise canine that symbolizes speed and dates back to 4,000 years ago; BORZOI, average weight 90 pounds, height 30 inches, the elegant, courageous, and agile Russian Wolfhound bred primarily for the hunt; SCOTTISH DEERHOUND, average weight 95 pounds, height 31 inches, possesses loyalty and devotion to his master or mistress and fine hunting instinct; ENGLISH FOXHOUND, average weight 70 pounds, height 24 inches, famous for foxhunting in packs in England; HARRIER, average weight 45 pounds, height 20 inches, a smaller edition of the Foxhound and known for hunting hares; COONHOUND, average weight 60 pounds, height 25 inches, bred for proficiency on possum and raccoon and capable of withstanding all types of weather; BASSET HOUND, average weight 50 pounds, height 14 inches, second only to the Bloodhound in trailing ability and possesses mild temperament; AFGHAN HOUND, average weight 60 pounds, height 27 inches, hails from Afghanistan and is known for racing and hunting, as well as a unique appearance; SMOOTH-HAIRED DACHSHUND, average weight 20 pounds, height 9 inches, the German name meaning "badger dog" and having the same characteristics as the Wire-haired.

HARRIER

BASSET HOUND

AFGHAN

COONHOUND

SMOOTH-HAIRED
DACHSHUND

HOUNDS

OTTERHOUND

WHIPPET

SALUKI

RHODESIAN RIDGEBACK

The OTTERHOUND has an average weight of 85 pounds and height of 25 inches; this hound hunts quarry on land and in water and has a rough coat and webbed feet. The SALUKI has an average weight of 60 pounds and height of 25 inches; this royal dog of Egypt has tremendous speed and can bring down gazelle and other quarry over deep sand and on rocky mountains. The WHIPPET has an average weight of 20 pounds and height of 20 inches; the Whippet has a quiet nature and denotes gracefulness, speed, and elegance. The RHODESIAN RIDGEBACK has an average weight of 70 pounds and height of 26 inches; this dog comes from Africa and has a distinctive ridge of hair which grows in the opposite direction down the middle of the back.

IRISH WOLFHOUND

The IRISH WOLFHOUND is the tallest of all dogs and has been used to hunt elk and wolves. The average weight is 130 pounds and the height is 34 inches. Height of a dog always is measured from the withers (highest point of the shoulder) to the ground. When an IRISH WOLFHOUND stands up on the hind legs, the dog is over 6 feet high. This dog has a gentle disposition and sense of companionship and requires a great deal of exercise. The Irish Wolfhound has a rough coat and a commanding appearance, a combination of power and swiftness, as the dog is muscular yet graceful. The breed has a proud heritage, and while alert and courageous, the Irish Wolfhound is not suspicious or aggressive. Hence, he is not a guard dog or watch dog. Bred to hunt and gallop with ease, he is calm, dignified, and sensitive. He is not to be confined, for he enjoys the chase and is well suited for coursing.

NORWEGIAN ELKHOUND

The NORWEGIAN ELKHOUND has an average weight of 50 pounds and height of 20 inches. Hunter of big game in his native Norway, the Elkhound was the comrade of the Vikings and possesses excellent stamina to perform in rugged conditions.

WORKING DOGS

BELGIAN SHEEPDOG

ALASKAN MALAMUTE

BERNESE MOUNTAIN DOG

BOXER

The BELGIAN SHEEPDOG has an average weight of 60 pounds and height of 23 inches; this breed has been used overseas as a police dog for many years. The BOXER has an average weight of 70 pounds, height 23 inches, and gets his name from the way he uses his paws when playing; ALASKAN MALAMUTE, average weight 85 pounds, height 24 inches, the Arctic sled dog with a fondness for people, especially children; BERNESE MOUNTAIN DOG, average weight 65 pounds, height 25 inches, the sturdy Swiss mountain dog.

BELGIAN TERVUREN

BRIARD

BOUVIER DES FLANDRES

GIANT SCHNAUZER

BELGIAN TERVUREN, average weight 55 pounds, height 24 inches, the untiring guardian of flocks; BOUVIER DES FLAN-DRES, average weight of 70 pounds, height 25 inches, a powerfully built dog with a rugged appearance; BRIARD, average weight 70 pounds, height 25 inches, the French herding dog with a distinctive look; GIANT SCHNAUZER, average weight 75 pounds, height 23 inches, a robust and courageous animal with a dense wiry coat.

WORKING DOGS

BULLMASTIFF

CARDIGAN WELSH CORGI

DOBERMAN PINSCHER

GERMAN SHEPHERD

BULLMASTIFF, average weight 120 pounds, height 26 inches, a fearless yet docile mixture of the Mastiff and the Bulldog; DOBERMAN PINSCHER, average weight 70 pounds, height 27 inches, a well-chiseled and muscular dog with a sleek coat; CARDIGAN WELSH CORGI, average weight 25 pounds, height 12 inches, a long and low-set herd dog with an alert expression; GERMAN SHEPHERD, average weight 75 pounds, height 25 inches, distinguished for loyalty, courage, intelligence, and the ability to train easily.

WORKING DOGS

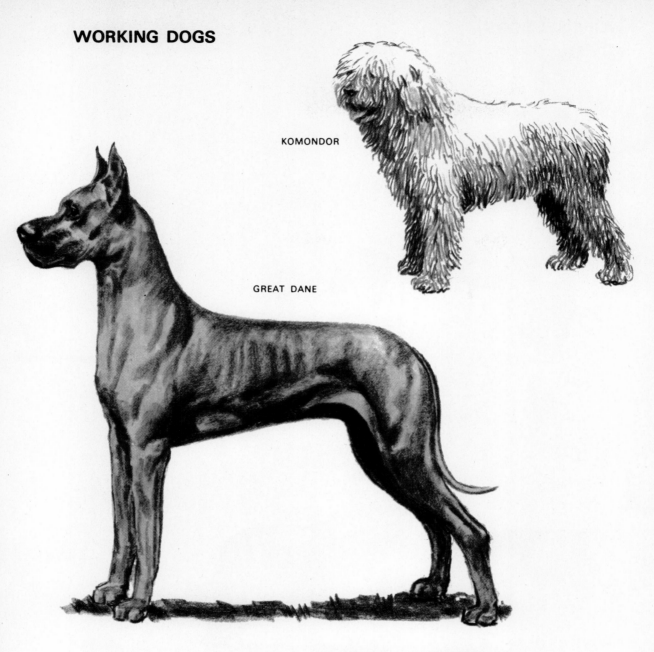

KOMONDOR

GREAT DANE

KOMONDOR, average weight 90 pounds, height 28 inches, the strong Hungarian protector of sheep and house-guardian with an unusual coat that protects him from the elements; GREAT DANE, average weight 130 pounds, height 32 inches, a friendly and dependable dog of the giant breeds.

WORKING DOGS

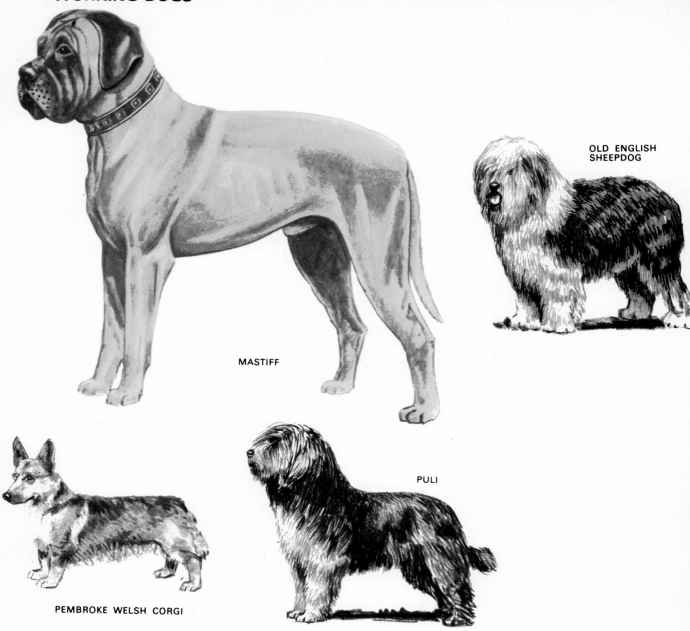

MASTIFF

OLD ENGLISH
SHEEPDOG

PULI

PEMBROKE WELSH CORGI

The number of dogs in the Working Group has more than doubled in recent years. The MASTIFF has been known in England for centuries. The dog's average weight is 185 pounds, height 32 inches, and this breed has hunted game such as lion. He is a massive watchdog with great power and agility, yet he is of good nature. PEMBROKE WELSH CORGI, average weight 25 pounds, height 11 inches, an affectionate, intelligent, and alert guardian of the home; OLD ENGLISH SHEEPDOG, average weight 95 pounds, height 24 inches, noted for his bearlike gait and compact body; PULI, average weight 35 pounds, height 17 inches, smallest of Hungarian sheepdogs and possessing a unique coat that appears unkempt.

SIBERIAN HUSKY

ST BERNARD

KUVASZ

GREAT PYRENEES

SIBERIAN HUSKY, average weight 50 pounds, height 22 inches, naturally friendly and not aggressive; ST. BERNARD, average weight 165 pounds, height 28 inches, the rescue dog with a keen sense of smell, pathfinding ability, and great strength; KUVASZ, average weight 70 pounds, height 26 inches, a white and sturdy dog with determination and intelligence; GREAT PYRENEES, average weight 115 pounds, height 30 inches, a dog of great majesty and kindly expression yet having marvelous instinct in snow and mountainous country.

WORKING DOGS

ROTTWEILER

SAMOYED

STANDARD SCHNAUZER

SMOOTH COLLIE

The ROTTWEILER is a splendid guard with a dignified demeanor. The average weight of this dog is 85 pounds, height 25 inches. STANDARD SCHNAUZER, average weight 35 pounds, height 19 inches, a squarely built dog with a dense and harsh coat; SAMOYED, average weight 55 pounds, height 22 inches, often called "the big white dog with the smiling face"; SMOOTH COLLIE, average weight 65 pounds, height 24 inches, has a short, flat coat with an abundance of undercoat but is otherwise similar to the Rough version.

COLLIE

SHETLAND SHEEPDOG

NEWFOUNDLAND

SHETLAND SHEEPDOG, average weight 16 pounds, height 14 inches, a small, rough-coated, long-haired dog sometimes referred to as the "Sheltie"; COLLIE, average weight 65 pounds, height 24 inches, a nicely proportioned dog with an abundance of coat; NEWFOUNDLAND, average weight 140 pounds, height 27 inches, a multipurpose dog on land and in water and has natural lifesaving instincts and a deep devotion to adults and children.

TERRIERS

AUSTRALIAN
TERRIER

DANDIE DINMONT
TERRIER

LAKELAND TERRIER

MANCHESTER

AIREDALE
TERRIER

BORDER TERRIER

CAIRN

COLORED BULL TERRIER

The Terrier Group includes many different dogs, with a wide range of sizes. The DANDIE DINMONT TERRIER has an average weight of 22 pounds and height of 10 inches, and the head and eyes are large while the body is long and low. The AIREDALE has an average weight of 50 pounds, height 23 inches, and is the largest of the terriers. BORDER TERRIER, average weight 14 pounds, height 12 inches, a working terrier that loves to "go to ground"; AUSTRALIAN TERRIER, average weight 12 pounds, height 10 inches, a sturdy, spirited, and grand little dog; LAKELAND TERRIER, average weight 16 pounds, height 14 inches, a self-confident little dog with a quiet disposition and excellent ability to tunnel underground; MANCHESTER, average weight 18 pounds, height 16 inches, a game little fellow with a sleek ebony coat; CAIRN, average weight 14 pounds, height 10 inches, named for the rocky piles into which he burrowed after game; Colored BULL TERRIER, average weight 50 pounds, height 20 inches, muscular and determined, but of sweet disposition.

BEDLINGTON TERRIER

MINIATURE SCHNAUZER

KERRY BLUE

SEALYHAM TERRIER

IRISH TERRIER

WIRE-HAIRED FOX TERRIER

BEDLINGTON, average weight 23 pounds, height 16 inches, a graceful dog with a gentle nature and a lightness of movement; KERRY BLUE TERRIER, average weight 35 pounds, height 18 inches, an all-round working and utility terrier with a soft, dense and wavy coat; IRISH TERRIER, average weight 27 pounds, height 18 inches, "the daredevil of terriers" with keen intelligence, a marvelous sense of humor, and a wonderful way with children; MINIATURE SCHNAUZER, average weight 15 pounds, height 13 inches, characterized by compact build, wiry coat, and abundant furnishings; SEALYHAM TERRIER, average weight 20 pounds, height 10 inches, an outgoing companion that is easily trained; WIRE-HAIRED FOX TERRIER, average weight 17 pounds, height 15 inches, a lively little dog with ears set high on the head.

SCOTTISH TERRIER, average weight 20 pounds, height 10 inches, a game terrier with a specific gait that is peculiarly his own; SKYE TERRIER, average weight 25 pounds, height 9 inches, a profusely coated dog that is twice as long as he is high; WEST HIGHLAND WHITE TERRIER, average weight 16 pounds, height 11 inches, determination and devotion in a little white body; STAFFORDSHIRE TERRIER, average weight 45 pounds, height 18 inches, a courageous, intelligent, smooth-coated terrier; white BULL TERRIER, average weight 50 pounds, height 20 inches, a gentle dog that is strongly built; WELSH TERRIER, average weight 20 pounds, height 15 inches, eyes set far apart in characteristic expression that is different from other terriers; SMOOTH FOX TERRIER, average weight 17 pounds, height 15 inches, flat, hard, dense coat and classic silhouette.

WEST HIGHLAND WHITE TERRIER

SCOTTISH TERRIER

STAFFORDSHIRE TERRIER

WELSH TERRIER

SKYE TERRIER

WHITE BULL TERRIER

SMOOTH FOX TERRIER

TOY DOGS

JAPANESE TOY SPANIEL

PEKINGESE

SMOOTH-COATED CHIHUAHUA

ITALIAN GREYHOUND

PAPILLON

SILKY TERRIER

YORKSHIRE TERRIER

BRUSSELS GRIFFON

TOY POODLE

PAPILLON, average weight 11 pounds, height 11 inches, an elegant dog with butterfly ears; SILKY TERRIER, average weight 9 pounds, height 9 inches, a native of Australia; ITALIAN GREYHOUND, average weight 10 pounds, height 13 inches, similar to the Greyhound but much smaller and more slender; BRUSSELS GRIFFON, average weight 8 pounds, height 8 inches, a real personality dog; PEKINGESE, average weight 9 pounds, height 6 inches, a regal and independent Oriental dog; SMOOTH-COATED CHIHUAHUA, average weight 4 pounds, height 5 inches, a clannish toy breed; YORKSHIRE TERRIER, average weight 6 pounds, height 8 inches, a very confident and intelligent breed; TOY POODLE, average weight 7 pounds, height 9 inches, the smallest of the three varieties of Poodle; JAPANESE TOY SPANIEL, recently recognized as the Japanese Chin.

NONSPORTING DOGS

ENGLISH TOY SPANIEL

LONG-COATED CHIHUAHUA

POMERANIAN

MALTESE

DALMATIAN

PUG

MINIATURE PINSCHER

AFFENPINSCHER

MANCHESTER TOY TERRIER

STANDARD POODLE

The ENGLISH TOY SPANIEL has an average weight of 10 pounds, height 10 inches, affectionate and intelligent little dog of royalty; LONG-COATED CHIHUAHUA, average weight 4 pounds, height 5 inches, a diminutive dog that is alert and clannish; PUG, average weight 16 pounds, height 10 inches, appears well groomed and has a roguish face; AFFENPINSCHER, average weight 8 pounds, height 10 inches, a fearless and devoted pal; POMERANIAN, average weight 5 pounds, height 7 inches, a vivacious yet docile little dog; MALTESE, average weight 6 pounds, height 6 inches, gentle and affectionate yet eager and sprightly; MINIATURE PINSCHER, average weight 8 pounds, height 11 inches, known as the "Minpin" and is an excellent watchdog with a sleek coat and lively temperament; TOY MANCHESTER TERRIER, a miniature replica of the Manchester Terrier.

The DALMATIAN has an average weight of 45 pounds, height of 21 inches, and is the original "coach dog" that naturally takes to horses. The STANDARD POODLE has an average weight of 55 pounds and height of 23 inches. This breed is elegant and intelligent, and the dog requires careful grooming in traditional fashion.

FRENCH BULLDOG

BOSTON TERRIER

SCHIPPERKE

KEESHOND

BULLDOG

MINIATURE POODLE

SHIH TZU

CHOW CHOW

LHASA APSO

FRENCH BULLDOG, average weight 22 pounds, height 12 inches, a muscular dog with bat ears; KEESHOND, average weight 40 pounds, height 18 inches, an ideal companion dog; SHIH TZU, average weight 15 pounds, height 10 inches, walks with tail carried gaily over the back; BOSTON TERRIER, average weight 19 pounds, height 14 inches, a native American breed; BULLDOG, average weight 50 pounds, height 15 inches, a symbol of courage worldwide; CHOW CHOW, average weight 60 pounds, height 20 inches, a powerful dog with untouched naturalness; SCHIPPERKE, average weight 15 pounds, height 12 inches, a faithful little watchdog; MINIATURE POODLE, average weight 16 pounds, height 13 inches, a fashionable pet; LHASA APSO, average weight 15 pounds, height 10 inches, an assertive dog with a tail upcurled over the back.

HOW TO CHOOSE THE BREED
THAT BEST SUITS YOU

A father was once faced with the task of selecting a puppy for his six-year-old son. Rather than risk buying a dog that the youngster wouldn't like, he allowed the lad to pick out his own pet. After studying the group of 10 puppies for an hour, the little boy finally exclaimed with joy, "Daddy, Daddy, get me that one!" pointing to a small puppy. "Which one?" asked his father. "That one, Daddy," he said, pointing to the tail-wagging puppy. *"I want the one with the happy ending!"*

Unfortunately, it may not be that easy for you to decide upon the puppy that you want. There are many things to consider. But first things first. *You should not buy a puppy on a whim.* You must be sure that your family members all agree that they desire a four-legged member of the family. You must remember that whatever breed you select, be it an expensive rare purebred pooch or a Heinz dog (a mixture of "57 varieties"), no two of which look alike, they require approximately the same food, care, training, grooming and attention. It is just as expensive to maintain a mutt as it is to keep a purebred dog.

If possible, buy a puppy between the ages of eight weeks and four months. It is advantageous to choose a puppy for three important reasons:

1. The puppy is not attached to anyone when you get him.
2. He is more easily trained.
3. You will have him with you longer.

When you select your breed, keep in mind the following:

1. Small dogs are well suited to small apartments.
2. Large dogs are more expensive to feed than small dogs.
3. Do not keep large breeds unless they can have an area large enough for them to get plenty of exercise. Dogs allowed loose are a menace and can be taken away from you by law if you do not maintain them properly.

As far as the external symptoms of an unhealthy pup are concerned, look for these:

1. Running eyes.
2. Cough.
3. Diarrhea.
4. Body temperature should be 102°F. if dog is normal.
5. Listlessness.
6. Red blotches on skin could be mange, ringworm, eczema or fungus.
7. Crooked legs means rickets.

When you buy your dog have an understanding that you will take your dog *immediately* to a veterinarian and, if he advises you that the dog is in poor condition, that you will have the right to return the dog (usually you will be required to have a note from the vet substantiating your claims).

Opposite:
Sound temperament and good health are the prime requisites in evaluating a pup. Proper socialization helps the young dog to adjust to a new environment and to accept other animals in that environment. A dog and a cat, for example, can get along for many years together, provided their relationship at first is given a little time, attention, and understanding.

Top to bottom:
Smooth-haired
Dachshund, Scottish
Terrier, yellow Labrador
Retriever.

Not every household has such an assortment of pets, but this scene shows a variety of animals that have been domesticated and obviously accept each other. No doubt the woman is the "pack leader," the authority figure whom the animals obey. To be in control, one must be firm yet kind and must have the respect and admiration of the animals. The pets, in turn, will follow the routine that is established by the leader.

Top to bottom:
German Shepherd,
Basset Hound, Pekingese

The Welsh Corgi puppies in this basket show the alert and foxy expression of the breed, and their future size can be predicted as approximately 11 inches high.

The eternal question of which is better, a male or female dog, certainly can be answered. It is an established fact that females are more lovable and affectionate than male dogs. Then again, male dogs have certain habits which make toilet training a bit more bothersome. Female dogs, as a general rule, are much easier to train, are more faithful and can have puppies (if you desire). With the female her only disadvantage is her "heat" period.

Every normal female dog has a certain period that occurs every six months or so. These periods last for about three weeks; during them a slight discharge occurs. It is during this time that she must be mated, and the proper time is usually about the tenth day after the start of flow. Naturally the female must be closely watched during these times, for she will not discriminate between male dogs when one is allowed near her. If it is your intention to breed her, you must select a suitable male. A purebred dog should be mated with another purebred dog of the same breed. Then pedigree papers and registration papers make the puppies that much more valuable. If you have a mixed breed dog, the selection of the stud dog is entirely open, for even if you have a small female and you mate her with a small male, there is no guarantee that the puppies will be small. It is the continuous inbreeding of pure lines that guarantees that if you mate two pure breeds you will get the same type as the parents. That's the advantage of spending a few dollars more to get yourself a purebred dog.

CARING FOR THE PUPPY

Don't forget that children always love small dogs, but when it comes to cleaning up after them or walking them for their relief and exercise, that may be a different story. Mother should be consulted here, for more often than not, the dog will be more her responsibility than anyone else's.

It is assumed that you have a place in mind to keep the dog. Either the dog will be kept in the house, in your cellar

Bringing Your Puppy Home

When you bring your puppy home, whether mongrel or purebred, you will need the following items to maintain him properly:

1. A harness and lead.
2. Food and a diet to follow.
3. A dog bed.
4. A suitable set of feeding dishes.
5. Toys to teethe on and play with.
6. Comb and brush.
7. Suitable bathing accessories.
8. Vitamin and mineral supplement.

THE HARNESS AND LEAD

Every puppy should be as full of life and pep as he can possibly be; as a matter of fact, that is one of the tests of a healthy dog. However, when it is time to take your puppy for a walk, it is important for him to behave himself while on a leash.

Harnesses are usually made of leather. Young puppies love to chew and if they can find nothing better, they will chew on the harness. A good hour-long chew will ruin a single leather harness.

Most puppies grow rather fast and in a month or two might easily outgrow a good harness, so maybe a cheaper harness would be more practical. The decision is up to you.

A harness is placed over the shoulders of a puppy. It is supposedly more humane than a collar which goes around a puppy's neck, but it is the experience of many dog lovers that a puppy is more easily trained with a collar than a harness.

A *lead* or *leash* is the piece of chain or leather that connects the puppy to you. It should be 4 to 6 feet long and durable. A light chain is very satisfactory and, depending upon the quality of the chain, can either be cheap or expensive. Since the lead can be used as long as it lasts, it is definitely advisable to spend a few extra dollars and get a good lead, one that will not break and will be comfortable for both yourself and the puppy.

This type of chain limits the amount of leverage around the dog's neck; the upper loop is attached to the lead.

FOOD FOR YOUR PUPPY

When you have bought your dog, the person you purchase him from should give you the diet he has been maintained on up to this time. Keep him on the same diet as long as recommended.

A puppy should be fed four times a day. In the morning give him some milk (not cold) with a little cereal or egg added (plus some vitamins and minerals). About noon feed him his heavy meal of dog food, cooked meat, egg biscuit or dry dog food mixed with milk, broth or water. About five in the afternoon give him a little more fine dog food or egg. Before you retire, some more milk should be offered.

Keep up this diet until the puppy is 3 or 4 months old, then gradually skip the evening milk. When the dogs is 6 or 7 months old he can be given the heavy meal in the evening and some milk fortified with vitamins and minerals in the morning. If your puppy doesn't seem to be thriving on this diet, have your veterinarian check him over and give you a more specific diet.

All food offered to your puppy should be clean and fresh, neither too hot nor too cold. Feed your puppy at the same time each day and remove whatever food he leaves behind. Don't allow the food to remain on the floor until he finally eats it. On the floor it gets dirty, dusty and stale, and you will soon have a sick puppy.

Once you have selected a brand of dog food, stick to it. Sometimes a change in diet will give a puppy loose bowels. The question is often asked: "Why is one dog biscuit so cheap and the other so expensive?" The answer is simple. Some dog food companies manufacture their biscuits as by-products from other sources. For example: some bakers when faced with a lot of stale bread sell it for grinding up and making dog biscuits. On the other hand, many dog food companies go out and buy top grade wheat. They prepare their dog biscuits according to a strict formula so that every time you buy their brand you get the same recipe. The latter type of dog food is naturally more expensive, but it is worth the difference because it will keep your dog healthier and happier.

Always look at the label and check the protein content of the dog food you buy. The higher the protein content, the more food content the dog can utilize (the remainder is mainly water and indigestible roughage and ash). Thus if "Brand A" sells for 25¢ per pound and has 25% protein, and "Brand B" is 40¢ per pound and has 50% protein, you are getting a bargain by buying the 40¢ brand. Your puppy would have to eat twice as much of "Brand A" to get the nutrition he needs. That's why some dogs are *always* eating (and having to relieve themselves). Remember: There is *more waste* in cheap dog food!

This Wire-haired Dachshund puppy knows that it is time to eat and is patiently waiting to receive his meal in his own special dish.

This Collie puppy is busily eating. Dogs do not thoroughly chew food; they tend to swallow it rapidly. Therefore, puppy food should be of the right consistency to help digestion.

Puppies can have the most expressive faces, as evidenced in this pair of Jack Russell Terriers. They are bright and alert, and they do not miss a sound. This particular type of terrier is quite game and is especially adept at "going to ground" for quarry. The Jack Russell Terrier is small, smart, and courageous.

The proper amount to feed a pup depends not only on the size of the breed but also on the temperament and the extent of exercise. Even puppies within a given litter, such as these yellow Labrador Retrievers, could have different requirements. Supplementary vitamins are important for growth and development.

VITAMIN AND MINERAL SUPPLEMENT

Regardless of how well you feed your dog, it is almost a certainty that your pet will not receive a balanced diet. To prevent any of the many dietary deficiency diseases to which most dogs fall prey at one time or another, you are advised to add a vitamin and mineral additive to the dog's diet. These are relatively inexpensive additives which will give your dog an ample supply of the rare ingredients that mean the difference between complete health and constant illness. This is especially true of breeding females that often suffer calcium deficiency after they are bred and while they are suckling their young.

Ask your pet supplier to recommend the supplements that are best suited for the dogs in your area. Requirements vary from one climate to another.

A PLACE FOR YOUR PUPPY TO SLEEP

Every dog likes to have a place that means *home*. To a dog there is nothing more sacred than his own little bed. Even a cardboard box with just a few torn newspapers will serve, as long as there is sufficient room for the puppy to stretch out. If you really want to make him feel like royalty, give your puppy a bed he will appreciate, a nice dog bed made especially for that purpose, with sweet-smelling cedar shavings in his mattress to keep the odor and the fleas away.

When you buy your puppy a bed make sure that it will be large enough to bed him comfortably when he is full grown. Ask your pet supplier to recommend the size best suited for your dog.

Locate your dog's bed on the floor away from drafts. A dark corner is good enough. Many people like to put the bed behind a chair where no one will see and disturb their sleeping puppy. Placing the bed near food is not a good idea because then your "Royal Puppy Highness" will get into the bad habit of taking his food into his bed to eat it. Feed him in a different room if possible.

If your puppy prefers to sleep with you instead of alone, you have no one but yourself to blame. The pup's first night in his new home is likely to be a memorable one for all. After spending five weeks of life with a bunch of cuddly fellow puppies and nice warm snuggly mother, he has been cruelly taken into a foreign environment, and now he has to sleep alone and be cold! However, you *must* be heartless that first night. Let him howl and cry. If you have a noisy alarm clock and an old doll, place them into his bed with him and let him sleep with some company. The alarm clock will make a comforting ticking noise and the doll will be something to snuggle. If you break down and take him into bed with you, he will keep you awake most of the night anyway, kissing your face and your feet, and you will then have started something that will be harder to correct the longer it continues.

A variety of dog beds can be found at pet shops. Here is a unique example of a dog bed that is manufactured by Crown Products.

FEEDING DISHES

All dogs, regardless of their breed, should be fed daily in the same set of dishes. Unless your breed is a special breed which requires specially shaped dishes to keep their ears out of the water and food, an ordinary dog dish will do. Since dogs eat by grasping the food with their teeth or lapping it up, they must eat from a dish which is securely moored to the floor, either by its own weight or by the friction legs of a food stand. If you do not have a fairly stationary dish, the dog will either tip the dish in his eagerness to feed or will push the dish against the nearest wall, possibly getting the wall dirty.

Ordinarily a dog needs two dishes—one for water which should be available at all times and one for food which should be filled at meal times, removed and washed immediately after the dog has eaten.

When selecting your doggie dishes keep three things in mind: 1. A good dish will last the lifetime of the dog. Don't buy a cheap thin pottery dish. Get a heavy plastic, metal or crockery dish or dinner set. 2. Get a dish large enough to comfortably hold the meal which will be necessary to feed your dog when he has matured. 3. Get a dish that can easily be cleaned, for you'll have to clean them every day!

TOYS FOR PLAY AND TEETHING

Puppies make interesting pets because they are playful, happy, loyal and lots of fun. But the owner of a puppy has certain responsibilities towards his puppy and one of them is to keep him occupied. Unless a puppy has proper teething toys, he will use your shoes, a corner of your best furniture or perhaps a piece of wood (like your favorite pipe). Biologically speaking, he simply MUST have something fairly hard to chew on to help him bring his teeth through his gums and to develop strong healthy teeth and gums.

Opposite:
This playful Miniature Poodle is ready to romp. A puppy is naturally active and inquisitive, but the animal should not be expected to play continuously, for a pup needs plenty of rest during the growing stage.

A dog has an instinctive need to chew, as this Brittany Spaniel tries to tell us, and he has a special need to keep his mouth occupied during the teething period which lasts until the age of 4 or 5 months.

YOUR DOG NEEDS TO CHEW

Puppies and young dogs need something with resistance to chew on while their teeth and jaws are developing—for cutting the puppy teeth, to induce growth of the permanent teeth under the puppy teeth, to assist in getting rid of the puppy teeth at the proper time, to help the permanent teeth through the gums, to assure normal jaw development and to settle the permanent teeth solidly in the jaws.

The adult dog's desire to chew stems from the instinct for tooth cleaning effect, gum massage and jaw exercise—plus the need for an outlet for periodic doggie tensions. In the veterinarian's book *Canine Behavior* published by *Canine Practice Journal*, Dr. Victoria L. Voith writes: "To reduce the dog's anxiety when left alone he should also be given a safety outlet such as a toy to play with and chew on. In fact, the dog may be encouraged to develop an oral attachment to this object by playing catch or tug of war with the toy at other times. Indestructible meat-flavored nylon bones are excellent."

Dental caries as it affects the teeth of humans is virtually unknown in dogs—but tartar accumulates on the teeth of dogs, particularly at the gum line, more rapidly than on the teeth of humans. These accumulations, if not removed, bring irritation, and then infection which erodes the tooth enamel and ultimately destroys the teeth at the roots. Most chewing by adult dogs is an effort to do something about this problem for themselves.

Tooth and jaw development will normally continue until your dog is more than a year old—but sometimes much longer, depending upon the breed, chewing exercise, the rate at which calcium can be utilized and many other factors, known and unknown, which affect the development of individual dogs. Diseases, like distemper for example, may sometimes arrest development of the teeth and jaws, which may resume months, or even years, later.

This is why dogs, especially puppies and young dogs, will often destroy property worth hundreds of dollars, when their chewing instinct is not diverted from their owner's possessions, particularly during the widely varying critical period for young dogs.

Saving your possessions from destruction, assuring proper development of teeth and jaws, providing for "interim" tooth cleaning and gum massage, and channeling doggie tensions into a non-destructive outlet are, therefore, all dependent upon your dog having something suitable for chewing readily available when his instinct tells him to chew. If your purposes, and those of your dog, are to be accomplished, what you provide for chewing must be desirable from the doggie viewpoint, have the necessary functional qualities, and above all, be safe for your dog.

Above and opposite:
Chewing is a natural action for dogs, especially young dogs; unfortunately, dogs don't always make the right decision about which articles are safe to chew, so it's up to the owner to be on guard and to provide safe, chewable items. The Nylabone being enjoyed by the Siberian Husky at left and the one being chewed by the Labrador Retriever above are safe and effective.

It is very important that dogs not be permitted to chew on anything they can break, or indigestible things from which they can bite sizeable chunks. Sharp pieces, from such as a bone which can be broken by a dog, may pierce the intestine wall and kill. Indigestible things which can be bitten off in chunks, such as toys made of rubber compound or cheap plastic, may cause an intestinal stoppage, if not regurgitated—to bring painful death, unless expensive surgery is promptly performed.

Strong natural bones, such as 4 to 8 inch lengths of round shin bone from mature beef—either the kind you can get from your butcher or one of the variety available commercially in pet stores—may serve your dog's teething needs, if his mouth is large enough to handle them effectively.

You may be tempted to give your puppy a smaller bone and he may not be able to break it at that time—but puppies grow rapidly and the power of their jaws constantly increases until maturity. This means that a growing dog may break one of the smaller bones at any time, swallow the pieces and die painfully before you realize what is wrong.

Many people make the mistake of thinking of their dog's teeth in terms of the teeth of the wild carnivores or those of the dogs of antiquity. The teeth of the wild carnivorous animals, and the teeth found in the fossils of the dog-like creatures of antiquity, have far thicker and stronger enamel than those of our contemporary dogs. Nature provides over the centuries only that which the animal needs to survive and procreate—and dogs have been domesticated for many thousands of years.

All hard natural bones are highly abrasive. If your dog is an avid chewer, natural bones may wear away his teeth prematurely; hence, they then should be taken away from your dog when the teething purposes have been served. The badly worn, and usually painful, teeth of many mature dogs can be traced to excessive chewing on natural bones.

Nylon bones, especially those with natural meat and bone fractions added, are probably the most complete, safe and economical answer to the chewing need. Dogs cannot break them or bite off sizeable chunks; hence, they are completely safe—and being longer lasting than other things offered for the purpose, they are economical.

Hard chewing raises little bristle-like projections on the surface of the nylon bones—to provide effective interim tooth cleaning and vigorous gum massage, much in the same way your tooth brush does it for you. The little projections are raked off and swallowed in the form of thin shavings—but the chemistry of the nylon is such that they break down in the stomach fluids and pass through without harmful effect.

The toughness of the nylon provides the strong chewing resistance needed for important jaw exercise and effective

Opposite:
The nylon bone fits comfortably in this Collie's mouth, for it slips across and just behind the canines. The canines are the four fangs, two upper and two lower, in the front part of the mouth. The smaller front teeth are called incisors.

help for the teething functions—but there is no tooth wear because nylon is non-abrasive. Being inert, nylon does not support the growth of micro-organisms—and it can be washed in soap and water, or it can be sterilized by boiling or in an autoclave. Many dogs, especially those whose teeth and gums have already been ravaged with poor-diet-induced degeneration, cannot chew the almost indestructible nylon bones. Your local petshop or veterinarian has a product (the only one presently on the market is called "Mytibone") made of softer material and which has 10% of its weight composed of real bone meal. This makes the bone softer and more palatable for the older dog who refuses the nylon bone or is unable to chew it because of the condition of its teeth and gums.

Nothing, however, substitutes for periodic professional attention to your dog's teeth and gums, not any more than your toothbrush can do that for you. Have your dog's teeth cleaned by your veterinarian at least once a year, twice a year is better—and he will be healthier, happier and far more pleasant to live with.

COMB AND BRUSH

Various breeds of dogs have completely different grooming requirements. Some dogs need constant combing and brushing to keep their coats in good repair and acceptable appearance. Wire-haired breeds need combing and brushing for everyday care and their grooming might require stripping equipment as well. Short-haired breeds might only require brushing and a comb would be of little value. When you buy your dog, inquire about what essential grooming tools are necessary—and make sure you use them!

Not only should a brush and comb be minimum requirements, but a proper dog-nail clipper is also essential, for dogs that are not allowed outdoors sufficiently grow long nails that must be trimmed periodically. Since their nails require extreme care in clipping due to the vein that runs through them, a special clipper has been developed which protects the vein from random snipping. The dog-nail clipper is a wise and small investment for the health of your dog.

SUITABLE BATHING ACCESSORIES

Most authors advise the dog owner to bathe their dogs only when absolutely necessary. This advice, in general, is well taken. But as with all generalizations, it is only practically applicable to dogs that spend the whole year out-of-doors. For outdoor dogs, the removal of thick hair coils might be dangerous to their survival in the cold winter nights, since the dense undercoat acts as a natural insulation and would otherwise be insufficient to keep the dog warm.

Opposite:
All grooming accessories should be kept in a special place that is handy for everyday use. Brushes, combs, scissors, etc. (as pictured opposite, above) can be put in a box or basket. Pictured (opposite, below) is a Lhasa Apso whose long, luxurious coat requires special attention. Dogs should accept as regular routine a few minutes of daily grooming, and it is best to start this procedure when the animal is a young puppy.

When bathing a dog, always be sure to rinse the coat thoroughly and then dry the ears in particular. This Beagle seems accustomed to his regular bath.

TOOLS

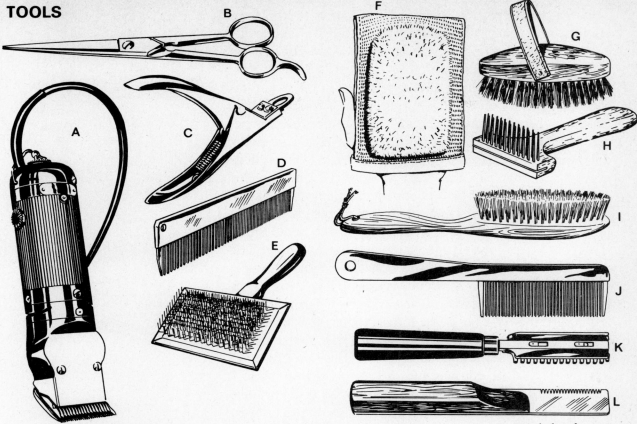

A—Small animal clipper.
B—7 inch scissor.
C—Nail Clipper.
D—Steel comb with two widths of teeth.

E—Carder or slicker brush.
F—Hound glove or mitt.
G—Bristle brush with wire center.
H—Rake.

I—Bristle brush.
J—Steel comb.
K—Dresser.
L—Stripping knife.

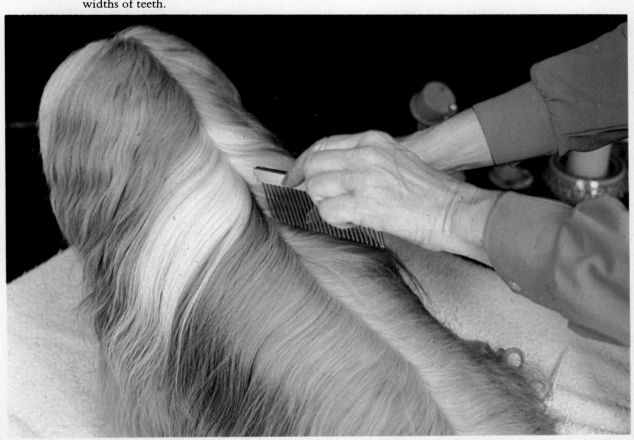

For the house pet, the doggy odor accentuated by the accumulation of dog hair oils might be offensive, and it is a necessity that the dog be free of body odors and that his coat be clean and shining.

Combing and brushing on a regular basis (a few minutes each day) greatly serves this purpose, and if the dog owner practices these essentials, there is little doubt that his pet can get along with 3 or 4 bathings a year. But how many dog owners are sufficiently disciplined to care for their dogs properly in this manner? Very few indeed and for this reason dogs require a bath about every month in the summertime and every two months in the wintertime.

When bathing your dog you need only a suitable dog shampoo, a heavy towel, a large tub and a strong back. The dog's bath is simple. Wet the dog thoroughly, using a plastic water glass to saturate his coat by pouring water over him while he stands in a few inches of warm water. It is assumed that you can bathe him in the bathtub or a large basin. After he has been thoroughly wet, add the shampoo or dog soap and work up a good lather. Then rinse him off the same way that you wet him down, being very careful that all of the soap has been taken from his coat. Be sure during the process that no soap gets into his mouth or eyes. His ears can be protected by stuffing them with cotton wadding.

After he has been thoroughly cleaned with two soapings and a thorough rinsing, you can lift him carefully from the bath while at the same time wrapping him in a towel. The dog's first reaction will be to shake the excess water from his coat with a violent shake. Unless he is covered with a towel and has had most of the excess water rubbed from his coat, expect a shower bath yourself from the water which will be shaken free by his typical shaking action.

In the wintertime it is safer to use one of the dry shampoos that are manufactured especially for dogs. Follow the instructions carefully.

If you are unable to bathe and groom your own dog, your veterinarian, kennel owner or petshop personnel will be able to tell you who will.

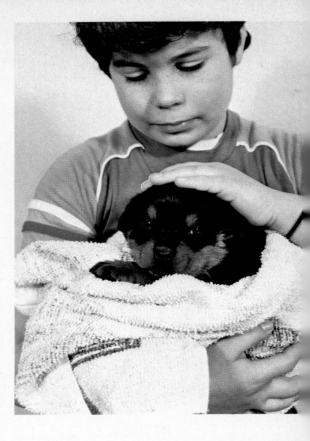

Above: A gentle rubbing with a heavy towel dries a pup and reassures the animal that all is well. *Below:* Some breeds, such as the Rottweiler (also shown above), take to water even at a very young age.

Opposite page:
The coat of a dog serves as insulation as exemplified by this Old English Sheepdog. Daily brushing helps to keep the coat clean.

Communication between pup (here a Pug) and master requires clear direction and response. Dogs have marvelous perception, and although they do not speak, they certainly can communicate.

How to Train Your New Puppy

It has often been stated that the difference between an "animal" and a "pet" is *training*. The obvious truth of this simple statement makes it imperative that you consider training your dog from the minute you own him. The first training is to teach him to sleep quietly in his own bed and not to disturb your own sleep. This was covered earlier.

The second most essential training is his toilet training. For the small dog that will spend most of his time indoors, toilet training is different from the larger dog that can be taken outside at any time. Small dogs, such as Chihuahuas, Pekingese and the like, can usually just as easily be trained to newspaper laid discreetly in the corner. This training is easily accomplished by using a housebreaking scent and putting the scent on some newspaper. The dog will be attracted to the scent and will get the general idea without much help from you.

Without a scent, or to supplement it, use some slightly soiled newspaper that has a bit of dog urine on it. Usually the dog will use that paper again and again. Once you replace it, the dog will have been accustomed to relieving himself on the paper. If you find him relieving himself in another location, then you must chastise him. Only do this when you catch him in the actual act. It doesn't take long to get the idea across.

For the outside dog, a dog that can be walked or let out into a fenced-in yard, the training is simpler. Immediately after every meal walk the dog until the dog relieves himself. As soon as he has made his toilet, reward him with an affectionate pat. It won't be too long before your dog understands what is expected of him and he will do it in a hurry.

For larger dogs that jump up to greet you every time you get home from shopping or work, the remedy is simple. As soon as the dog jumps, just bend your knee so it catches him in the chest as he jumps at you. Naturally he will be knocked off balance. It only takes a few days—and a few jumps—for this behavior to end.

Boxers as we know them today were first bred in Munich, Germany, about one hundred years ago. Medium-sized yet strong and heavily built, our present-day Boxers make ideal guardians whose intelligence, stamina, and great courage cannot be denied. Perhaps this is why so many families with young children keep Boxers as pets; they are great protectors of their home and family.

If you have a dog that is a "barker" and you don't want him to bark (often people buy "barkers" to scare away thieves or intruders), merely reprimand him every time he starts barking. This will stop in time, but there are some dogs that can never be stopped from barking.

While walking your dog, be sure that there is an understanding between you and the dog as to who is the boss. Don't allow him to pull you in all directions. It is easy to train your dog to walk properly on the lead by holding the dog very close to your feet on a short leash. If he wants to pull, jerk him back with a sharp HEEL! A light slap on the snoot with your finger will emphasize that he shouldn't pull. It takes but a few long walks to have your dog walking closely beside you on a leash, and finally he will do the same on a loose lead.

The education of your dog is far from complete if he is merely housebroken and knows how to walk on a lead. If you want an animal that you can own with pride, you must train him in other fields. Training your dog intellectually distinguishes you from the next person, and your dog will only be as intelligent as you want him to be. Understand that your dog does not speak the same language that you do and that training is a long, repetitious process requiring a constant use of the same hand and word command. If you are to be a success with your dog, you must actually learn to think as your dog thinks. Dogs do things solely from their own point of view. There must be some reason for your dog to act the way he does. With this in mind you must place your dog in situations that are such that he cannot get out of them without doing as you desire. For example, if you want him to keep off the furniture, you must teach him to sit at your feet in the living room and to follow you wherever you go. When you allow him into the room, scold and punish him severely when he jumps on the chairs; but when he sits at your feet, pet him gently and talk in a low, reassuring voice. It is not long before he learns what will reward him and what will result in punishment. This same treatment works for all social graces.

Remember: When you punish your dog, you must do so while the dog is in the actual act of disobedience. If you punish him later, he will not understand you and this will add greatly to his confusion.

Once you've taught him a few things by this method (and you can start by training him to come when he hears his name or when you whistle), other things will be easy. Keep up the training during the first three or four months that you have the dog and the training will be easier and easier. Let the training go for a few weeks and you must just about start from scratch.

What To Do If Your Dog Becomes Ill

No book can teach you how to treat an illness of your dog. Not only is there the problem of treatment of the disorder, but there is a problem in properly diagnosing the illness. If your dog should become ill or manifest any of the symptoms of a particular disease, do not waste time. Contact a veterinarian immediately.

IMPORTANCE OF INOCULATIONS

To keep your dog protected as much as possible from major diseases, maintain a routine series of inoculations.

Distemper

Young dogs are most susceptible to distemper, although it may affect dogs of all ages. Signs of the disease are loss of appetite, depression, chills and fever, as well as a watery discharge from the eyes and nose. Unless treated promptly, the disease goes into advanced stages with infections of the lungs, intestines and nervous system. Dogs that recover may be impaired with paralysis, convulsions, a twitch or some other defect, usually spastic in nature. Early inoculations in puppyhood should be followed by an annual booster to help protect against this disease.

Hepatitis

The initial symptoms of hepatitis are drowsiness, vomiting, loss of appetite, high temperature and great thirst. Often these symptoms are accompanied by swellings of the head, neck and abdomen. This disease strikes quickly, and death may occur in only a few hours. An annual booster shot is needed after the initial series of puppy shots.

Leptospirosis

Infection is begun by the dog's licking substances contaminated by the urine or feces of infected animals, and the disease is carried by bacteria that live in stagnant or slow-moving water. The symptoms are diarrhea and a yellowish-brownish discoloration of the jaws, teeth and tongue, caused by an inflammation of the kidneys. A veterinarian can administer the leptospirosis shot along with the distemper and hepatitis shots.

Opposite:
Unusual behavior is a signal that something may be wrong in the health of a dog. After professional diagnosis by a veterinarian, the actual nursing of a sick dog can be taken care of at home. Familiar surroundings, warmth, cleanliness, and quiet help to speed recovery.

Rabies

This disease of the dog's central nervous system spreads by infectious saliva which is transmitted by the bite of an infected animal. Of the two main classes of symptoms, the first is "furious rabies," in which the dog shows a period of melancholy or depression, then irritation and finally paralysis. The first period can last from a few hours to several days, and during this time the dog is cross and will change his position often, lose his appetite, begin to lick, and bite or swallow foreign objects. During this phase the dog is spasmodically wild and has impulses to run away. The dog acts fearless and bites everything in sight. If he is caged or confined, he will fight at the bars and possibly break his teeth or fracture his jaw. His bark becomes a peculiar howl. In the final stage, the animal's lower jaw becomes paralyzed and hangs down. He then walks with a stagger, and saliva drips from his mouth. About four to eight days after the onset of paralysis, the dog dies.

The second class of symptoms is referred to as "dumb rabies" and is characterized by the dog's walking in a bearlike manner with his head down. The lower jaw is paralyzed, and the dog is unable to bite. It appears as if he has a bone caught in his throat.

If a dog is bitten by a rabid animal, he probably can be saved if he is taken to a veterinarian in time for a series of injections. After the symptoms appear, however, no cure is possible. The local health department must be notified in the case of a rabid dog, for this is a danger to all who come near him. As with the other shots each year, an annual rabies inoculation is very important.

Parvovirus

This relatively new virus is a contagious disease that has spread in almost epidemic proportions throughout certain sections of the United States. It has appeared also in Australia, Canada and Europe. Canine parvovirus attacks the intestinal tract, white blood cells and the heart muscle. It is believed to spread through dog-to-dog contact, and the specific source of infection seems to come from fecal waste matter of infected dogs. Overcoming parvovirus is difficult, for it is capable of existing in the environment for many months under varying conditions and temperatures, and it can be transmitted from place to place on the hair and feet of infected dogs, as well as on the clothes and shoes of people.

Vomiting and severe diarrhea, which will appear within five to seven days after the animal has been exposed to the virus, are the initial signs of this disease. At the onset of illness, the feces will be light gray or yellow-gray in color, and the urine might be blood-streaked. Because of the vomiting and severe diarrhea, the dog that has contracted the disease

Opposite:
The good health of a pup is in the hands of the owner. Careful attention, coupled with proper action, often can prevent an illness from progressing to a serious stage. It is obvious from this West Highland White Terrier's clear, shiny eyes and his alert expression that his owner has given him good care.

will dehydrate quickly. Depression and loss of appetite, as well as a rise in temperature, can accompany the other symptoms. Death caused by this disease usually occurs within 48 to 72 hours following the appearance of the symptoms. Puppies are hardest hit, and the virus is fatal to 75 percent of the puppies that contact it. Death in puppies can be within two days of the onset of the illness.

A series of shots administered by a veterinarian is the best preventive measure for canine parvovirus. It is also important to disinfect the area where the dog is housed by using one part sodium hypochlorite solution (household bleach) to thirty parts of water and to keep the dog from coming into contact with the fecal matter of other dogs.

INTERNAL PARASITES

Four common internal parasites that may infect a dog are: roundworms, hookworms, whipworms and tapeworms. The first three can be diagnosed by laboratory examination, and tapeworms can be determined by seeing segments in the stool or attached to the hair around the tail. When a veterinarian determines what type of worm or worms are present, he then can advise the best treatment. A dog in good physical condition is less susceptible to worm infestation than a weak dog. Proper sanitation and a nutritious diet help in preventing worms. One of the best preventive measures is to have clean, dry bedding for the dog, for this diminishes the possibility of reinfection due to flea or tick bites.

Heartworm infestation in dogs is passed by mosquitoes. Dogs with this disease tire easily, have difficulty in breathing and lose weight despite a hearty appetite. Administration of preventive medicine throughout the spring, summer and fall months is advised. A veterinarian must first take a blood sample from the dog to test for the presence of the disease; if the dog is heartworm-free, pills or liquid medicine can be prescribed to protect against any infestation.

Opposite:
Dogs have a natural inclination to relax and recline in the sunshine, as suggested by this pair of Golden Retrievers. Regular check-ups and routine inoculations help a dog to maintain top condition.

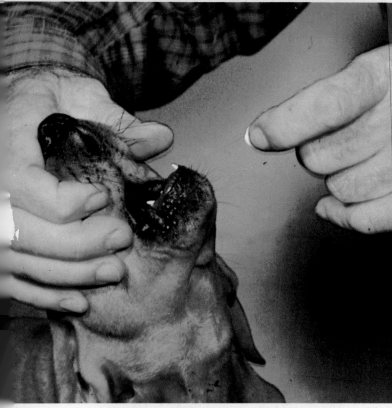

To give a capsule, open the dog's mouth by placing your hand around the foreface and pressing both sides of the dog's mouth.

Hold the dog's head back and place the capsule as far back on the tongue as you can reach. Remove your hand, close the mouth, and stroke the neck.

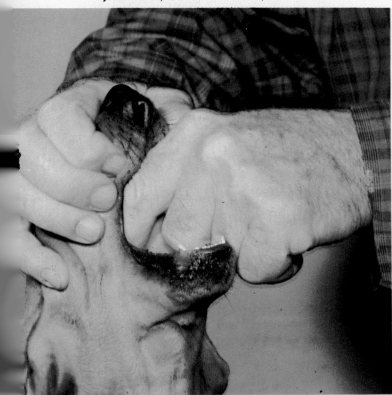

three or four feet long, depending on the size of the dog. Make a loop in the middle of the strip and slip it over his nose with the knot under his chin and over the bony part of the nose. Pull it tight and bring the ends back around his head behind the ears and tie it tightly, ending with a bow knot for quick, easy release.

Now you can handle the dog safely.

Should he attempt to get up and fight the mouth tie, you may have to tie his front legs together, and his back ones, or you could be severely scratched.

Occasionally a large dog goes beserk. How then can he be handled? You can make a lasso with a rope and throw the loop over his neck. If this doesn't control him, make another and throw that loop over his head also. Then one rope can be tied to some solid object, the other pulled tight by an assistant while you take hold of his collar. If he is not too large, try to jump and straddle his shoulders and then pull up on the collar. Now the ropes can be relaxed and your assistant can apply the mouth tie described above. The head of a large powerful dog can be pulled up snugly to a fence by passing the end of his leash through a hole in the fence, and his mouth tie can then be applied.

Should you have to keep your dog lying on his side because of broken bones or other injuries, hold his head down with one hand and with the other pull the hind legs out straight to the side; he can't get up unless he gets his legs under him.

HOW TO GIVE REMEDIES

To watch some dog owners giving pills, capsules or liquids to their pets, one would think it a great effort. It is not—when one goes about it forearmed with knowledge.

Giving capsules or pills: I have not suggested the use of any capsules or pills for the first aid emergencies in the following pages. However, your veterinarian may suggest using them if you have telephoned him for instructions, so here is the way they can be most easily given.

Presuming that you are right-handed, with your left hand place your palm over the dog's foreface and take hold of his lips, pressing them over the teeth with your

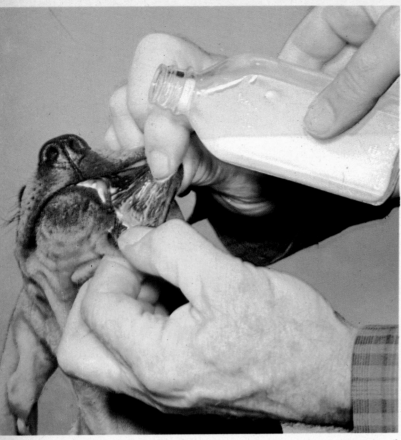

To administer liquid medicine, spread the side of the dog's mouth, form a lip pocket (above), and let the liquid trickle past the tongue. Allow time for the dog to swallow in small quantities.

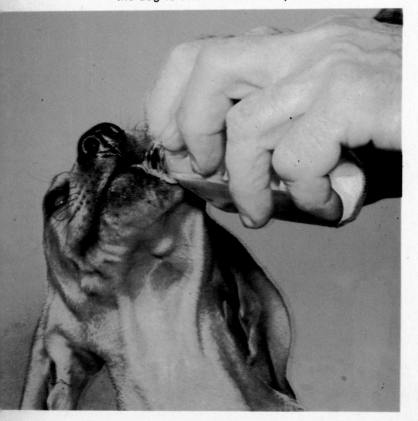

thumb on one side and fingers on the other. He will open his mouth.

Twist your wrist so his head is turned upward.

With your right hand pick up the capsule or pill between your index and second fingers. Keep your thumb out of the way.

Quickly slide the capsule over the back of the slippery tongue and push downward as far as your fingers can reach. Let go and withdraw your fingers. Snap the jaws together and watch for a movement of the dog's tongue. You will see him swallow. Watch to determine that he makes no motion to chew or spit the capsule out. It sometimes helps to massage his throat.

Inexperienced persons try to give capsules or pills holding them with thumb and index fingers. It is not possible in that way to push the capsule far enough back over the tongue for the dog to swallow it. So you understand now why the above instructions were given.

Administering liquids: Have your dog sit. Insert the first two fingers of your left hand into the angle of the lips on the dog's right side. Some people find it more natural to use their thumb and index fingers. Spread the lips apart, pulling them slightly outward from the teeth, forming a pocket or funnel. Try not to elevate the head higher than a line drawn between chin and eye parallel to the ground.

Now, with the right hand tip the container holding the liquid and pour an ounce into the lip pocket, holding the dog's head slightly upward. The liquid will trickle past the tongue and he will swallow. Remain at the side, never in front of the dog, as he may cough and spray you with the liquid. When he has swallowed, give more and continue until he has taken it all.

In the case of peroxide, try to give the full dose all at once, because when it begins to fizz in the throat he may fight against taking more.

Should your dog be lying down and you are giving him liquids as a stimulant, try to roll him up enough so that swallowing will be natural; otherwise the liquid may enter his windpipe, with tragic results.

SHOCK

A dog in any accident, especially one involving a blow to the head or one in which some vital organ is damaged or ribs broken, will generally, mercifully, go into shock. He is less conscious of pain, but his condition is frightening. His pulse and respirations are slow, and they may be very shallow. He may feel cold to the touch.

Don't try to apply a lot of heat. The best treatment is to cover him with blankets and let his own body heat build up. He will then recover slowly and naturally. While he is in shock you may be able to get him to a veterinarian who will sedate him when the state of shock disappears and the dog becomes more conscious of his pains. A veterinarian has equipment to help him relieve shock. He may give oxygen or even use an artificial respirator. So if possible hurry the dog to him.

To handle a small dog you can fold a blanket into several thicknesses, drop it over his back and manage him by holding him within it.

If the dog is small and in shock, it is better to pick him up by holding one hand under the front, the other under the hindquarters. This will keep him stretched out.

It is always better to roll an injured dog than to try to lift him. Suppose you find him lying beside the road after a car accident. Apply a mouth tie even if you have to use your necktie to make one. Send someone for a blanket. Spread the blanket out and roll him gently over on it. Two people, one on each side, can make a stretcher out of the blanket and move the dog easily.

If no blanket is available and the injured dog must be moved, try to keep him as flat as possible. So many dogs' backs are broken in car accidents that one must think first of that possibility. Once he is out of harm's way, if he can move his hind legs or tail, his spine is probably not broken.

A blanket or coat also is important in the case of shock, for the dog must be kept warm. In such cases the blanket or coat can act as both an improvised stretcher and as a provider of needed warmth.

Gently roll an injured dog onto a blanket or coat to be used as a stretcher, and calmly carry the dog so that no further injuries are caused. If possible, contact a veterinarian's office immediately to give advance notice that you are on the way with an emergency so that the vet will be ready for you and the dog when you arrive.

FIRST AID AND DRUGS

There are certain simple home remedies to be used as first aid accessories. Here are some that can be found in most households, together with doses and how to administer them. The doses given are for medium-size dogs. Give more or less according to the size of your dog.

3% hydrogen peroxide: Useful in cleaning wounds. When applied to contaminated areas it produces a fizzing that stops when the peroxide loses its strength. This drug is probably the best and simplest emetic known. The ordinary drugstore strength mixed with an equal amount of water and given by the lip pocket method, so a dog has to swallow it, will cause him to vomit in about two minutes. If he does not, repeat in five minutes. Moreover, peroxide is an antidote for a rather common poison—phosphorus. Dose: 2 ounces of the mixture (50/50 water and peroxide).

Epsom salts: This is a good physic and also an antidote for arsenic poisoning. Dose: 1 teaspoonful of Epsom salts in 2 ounces of water given via the lip pocket method.

Table salt: An antidote for thallium poisoning. Also a fair emetic in an emergency. Dose: 1 heaping teaspoonful in ⅓rd glass of water given via the lip pocket method.

Bicarbonate of soda: This is to be used in acid poisoning and is given by mouth. For acid burns on the body or feet it is applied in a strong solution. Dose (by mouth): a rounded teaspoonful in 2 ounces of water.

Vinegar or lemon juice: The acid content can be effective to neutralize caustics or alkalis. Dose: 2 ounces.

Coffee: A remarkable heart and kidney stimulant. It is quite long lasting. Dose: 1 heaping teaspoonful of instant coffee in a half cup of water.

Egg white: Antidote for mercury poison. Dose: the whites of six eggs after inducing vomiting.

Karo syrup (glucose): Give this to save dogs which have eaten certain poisonous plant leaves. Dose: 2 tablespoonfuls mixed with 3 ounces of water.

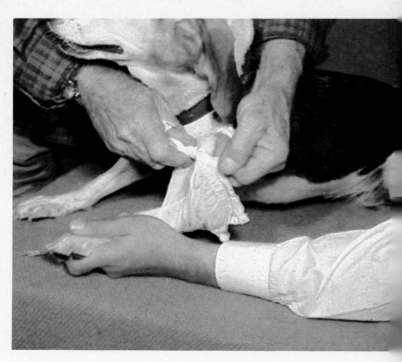

In applying a tourniquet to arrest bleeding, two people are needed; one person should hold the dog still, and the other should tie the bandage and twist it tightly with a stick. The people should be as calm as possible in order to reassure the dog and to maintain the dog's cooperation.

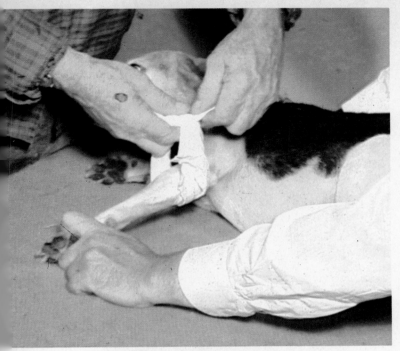

The dog can be defensive when injured, but if the animal senses that you are in control of the situation, it will realize that you mean well and will allow you to help.

Warmth, kindness, and understanding are important when aiding an injured dog, for the animal does not know what you are doing and must be made to feel that you are helping, not hurting.

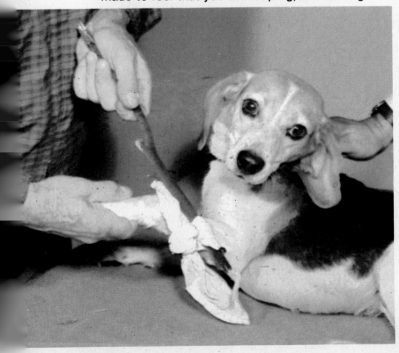

Mineral oil: This is to be used to relieve constipation. Dose by mouth: 2 teaspoonfuls.

Artificial respiration

After an accident, a dog is sometimes unable to breathe. Should yours be in this condition, first pull his tongue out; if he is unconscious, wipe out his throat with cotton or your handkerchief. Feel for a heart beat and if there is one try gently pressing on the rib cage and quickly releasing the pressure. Repeat many times. Stop as soon as you see or feel him breathing normally. This procedure has saved many a dog.

ELECTRIC SHOCKS, DROWNING, HEAT

A live wire on the floor offers a temptation to any dog and especially to puppies. If one chews the wire his mouth is usually burned, sometimes severely. He generally urinates and if he is standing close enough to a floor radiator or to a hot water or steam radiator which the urine touches, he may well be electrocuted. This doesn't mean he will die, but you can enhance his chances of living by quick first aid.

Keep away from the urine and shut off the switch which feeds the wire he has chewed. If you rush to his aid you too can be severely shocked. If you can't shut off the current, as for example when the wire is attached to a wall plug, then get a wooden cane or any dry wooden object—a broom, for example—and remove the wire from the dog's mouth.

Watch him to see if he is breathing. If not, feel his heart to determine whether it is still beating. If it is, give artificial respiration. Even if you cannot feel a heart beat try to revive him. Press down on the rib cage and suddenly release the pressure. Repeat at ten second intervals. Stop occasionally to see whether he is breathing naturally. When natural respiration starts, discontinue your treatment.

He will be in shock. Treat him accordingly. If the tongue and lips are burned, take him to his vet. Sometimes burns which would disfigure him for life can be treated and sutured effectively, especially burns on the lips.

There are other ways in which dogs can be electrocuted. They may chew Christmas tree ornaments with electric connections or be struck by lightning, but shock is usually the result.

Drowning

This is a rare occurrence, but first aid is usually needed for the unexpected. Dogs occasionally fall or are pushed off bridges by mischievous children. The impact against the water has been known to cause unconsciousness, or possibly the head has struck against a submerged object, and the dog may drown. Dogs apparently drowned do not always need to die if you will render artificial respiration.

The first thing you must do is pull out the dog's tongue and shake his head in a lowered position to drain the excess water out. In all of this, the speed with which you work is very important.

Heat stroke

Remember that the only appreciable way a dog has of reducing his temperature is by evaporating water from his throat and tongue. When water evaporates it becomes very cold at the point of evaporation. To reduce a helpless dog's temperature toward normal you must put this principle to work.

Suppose that you find your dog panting and slobbering and in a state of collapse. How should you give first aid? The quickest way is to put him in the bathtub and run cold water over him. You may be away from home. No bathtub. No hose in the back yard with which to wet him. Now what? Get some cold water, pour it over him and fan him to cause the water to evaporate. A newspaper or a wide board can be used as a fan and this will work, provided you put sufficient energy behind it and keep wetting him.

But suppose you are driving when the heat stroke occurs—a very frequent occurrence. Now what? Stop and get some water, if only a pint or quart, and after putting your dog on the floor of the front seat, open the cowl ventilator and let the air flow over him while you keep pouring enough water on his body to keep him damp. This nearly always

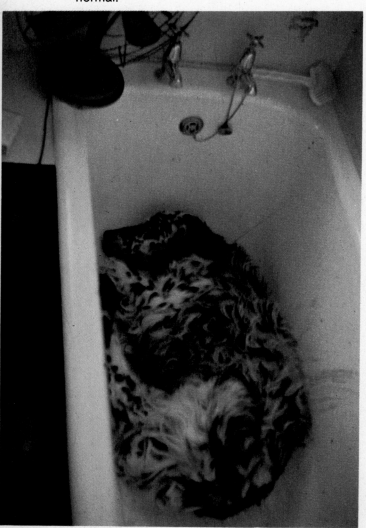

Improper ventilation can cause heatstroke. When air supply is limited, breathing is difficult and rapid, and the dog reaches a state of collapse. First aid includes a cool shower, cool wet towels, or a cool tub bath if available. The dog's temperature must be reduced and brought back to normal.

revives a dog. If you are travelling across a desert or in the deep South and your dog can't stand the heat, be sure to go prepared with some containers of water.

Needless to say, any heat-struck dog should be moved out of the sun and out of dead air pockets to a place where the breeze can ventilate him.

Since dogs reduce their temperature via their throats, it was long believed that dogs with extra heavy coats were insulated against heat as well as against cold. This notion, however, has not proved correct. Today we know that, except in the case of show dogs, it is better for his comfort to have him sheared all over. The hair will grow in again and the chances of heat stroke are much less than when the heavy coat is left on all summer.

HEART ATTACKS, CONVULSIONS

Old dogs often show typical symptoms of heart attacks. If your dog seems weak and prefers to lie down; if, when he stands, he tends to hold his legs farther apart than usual; if he pants, or after climbing the stairs seems to have trouble in breathing, he may be suffering from a heart attack.

Put your index finger against the inside of a hind leg, as high up as possible; you will feel the femoral artery pulsing. In a heart attack this pulse may be only barely palpable. Likewise, by placing your ear on the left side of the dog's chest behind the elbow, you may hear the heart beating feebly.

On the other hand your veterinarian may find instead of a heart attack an inherited defect or heart worms which live in the heart and which in large numbers produce symptoms similar to those of a heart attack. *Treatment:* If rest does not quickly permit your dog to overcome his weakness, try giving coffee with sugar and cream and giving it to him three or four times a day.

Convulsions

Before vaccinations against several once common diseases of the distemper complex were effective, convulsions in dogs were a much more common occurrence than they are today.

Periodic examination of the dog's mouth can prevent future problems in teeth and gums. Simply hold the foreface of the dog, lift the lips, and look at the inside of the mouth. As a dog grows older, the mouth should be checked regularly for loose teeth and gum disorders.

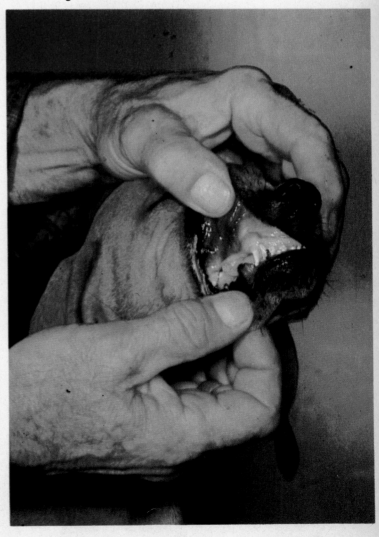

Convulsions often indicate epilepsy or they may, in puppies, be due to lumps of very coarse food in the stomach; but usually the convulsions indicate brain inflammation, often as a result of some virus disease. Very often the outcome will be unfavorable. Hardpad disease, for example, may not affect the dog very severely; but when the footpads begin to peel, convulsions may begin. The dog usually froths at the mouth and becomes rigid. He also usually defecates and urinates. Many die but some recover. As he recovers from an attack, the dog is usually dizzy. This is not rabies; a rabid dog does not recover. *Treatment:* Do not pick up a convulsive dog. Have faith that he will soon be over it. Clean him up and take him to the veterinarian where you can leave him for diagnosis and treatment. He may be on a downhill course. He may recover naturally or he may be left with a twitch in some groups of muscles, depending upon what area in his brain is damaged.

Certainly you do not want him having repeated convulsions at home, so unless his veterinarian advises you that he is better off at home let him manage the pet's treatment.

CUTS AND WOUNDS

First aid in these accidents consists of stopping the bleeding, cleaning the wound and preventing infection. A small amount of bleeding is often desirable as it washes away some impurities. When skin is torn leaving a raw area and is left untreated for even twenty-four hours, it will shrink and be difficult to stretch back into place when the veterinarian attempts to cover the raw area by suturing the skin.

If you cannot quickly reach his veterinarian, try to clean out the wound. Gently swab out any dirt or grease, and flood the area with peroxide to help loosen the foreign matter. If there is a flap of skin which you can draw across the area, do so, and gently bandage it in place, thus keeping the skin moist.

If the damaged area is not large, letting the dog lick it clean is one of the best possible treatments. He will remove the foreign matter, and the rough tongue surface will rid the

Just as a dog will lick a wound to heal it, the people helping a wounded dog should cleanse the cut and remove all foreign matter. One person should hold the dog's head so that the animal is looking in another direction while the other person is examining and cleaning the wound.

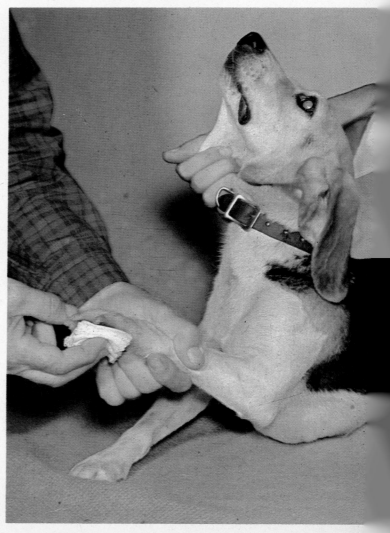

wound of all dead tissue. When he is finished, pull the skin flap over and bandage the area.

Removing splinters

Dogs, like human beings, are frequently pierced by splinters, the difference being that with dogs splinters usually penetrate their feet. If you see a dog limping or running on three legs, especially if he chews at the lame foot, examine the foot carefully. If you locate the splinter or other sharp object, tie his mouth and try to pull the object out with tweezers. If it does not come out, call in the veterinarian. Splinters left in the flesh too long can cause tetanus (lockjaw), especially if pus develops. The veterinarian will know whether the dog should be given antitoxin.

Not all splinters enter the feet. The dog will help you locate the offender by trying to pull it out himself.

Elastic bands

Mischievous children frequently put elastic bands around dogs' necks, ears, tails and legs, and the bands may go unsuspected until they have actually cut into or through the skin. Generally an obnoxious odor is the signal. The cut will ooze and attract flies. When elastic bands have been left on too long, ears and tails have actually fallen off.

First aid consists of hooking out the elastic and cutting it, pulling it from its bed and trying to clean out the area. This is often a tedious job because hair may have been pressed into the cut by the band, and dirt may have accumulated. There is usually a great deal of suturing to be done, so let your veterinarian handle the work properly as soon as possible.

FIRST AID IN POISONING

There are some basic facts you should understand about poisoning. There are many kinds of poisons. Some, like thallium, can act slowly or very quickly, depending on the amount ingested. Some, like cyanide, act so fast that saving a dog is impossible. You will recall having read in detective stories where a person drinking a potion with cyanide in it dies before he has finished the contents of the glass.

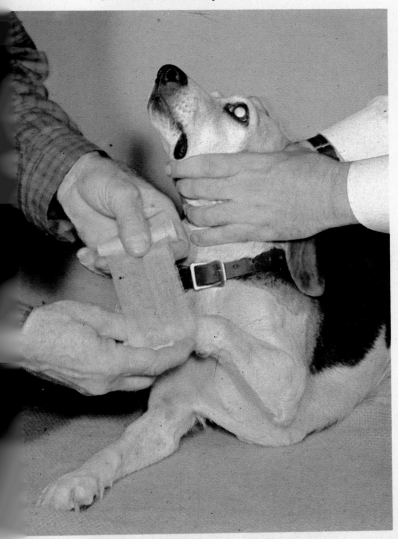

Speak calmly to a dog as you gently, yet tightly, bandage a wound. The dog will have a natural curiosity about how you are helping and will want to sniff and possibly pull away, so be sure that the animal is held firmly.

When poisoning is suspected try to determine what poison is involved. If you see your dog dig up a mole poison you have planted in a mole burrow, quickly find the container from which you took the poison bait and read the composition. By knowing the poison you can supply the antidote and treatment. In almost all cases, the first thing to do is empty the dog's stomach.

Sometimes a neighbor has been using poison. Should your dog swallow some, hurry to the neighbor and get him to read the composition of the toxic drug and the antidote. It may be some poison which you will not find mentioned here. Read the antidote, which is always listed on the package.

Whole books dealing with poisons have been published. Obviously we can consider only the more common ones here. If you suspect that your dog has been poisoned, phone your veterinarian for instructions.

Some poisons are corrosive; they burn what they touch—mouth, throat, gullet, stomach. In such cases, unless almost immediate antidotes are given, it is too late to help. Because the stomach contains fluid, the damage done by some acids and alkalis is not quite as immediate as the same corrosives would be if poured over the skin of your forearm, for example. The way to counteract their damage is to neutralize them by trying to keep the poisons from corroding deeper into tissue.

It is equally important to remember that once an area has been damaged, it requires a long time to heal. The dog may be unable to eat for weeks, yet still be alive when his organs have healed. Imagine a large area of your skin burned by a strong acid. How many weeks will it be before the area has healed and skin has grown slowly across to cover it? While the dog is recuperating from a poisoning case this fact must be taken into consideration. I assume that you will try to give first aid and then hustle your pet to the veterinarian. Don't expect him to wave a wand and all the tissues will be healed. No, they will take time and you must be a patient nurse during the healing process.

The following common poisons are listed in the order of their prevalence in my own experience.

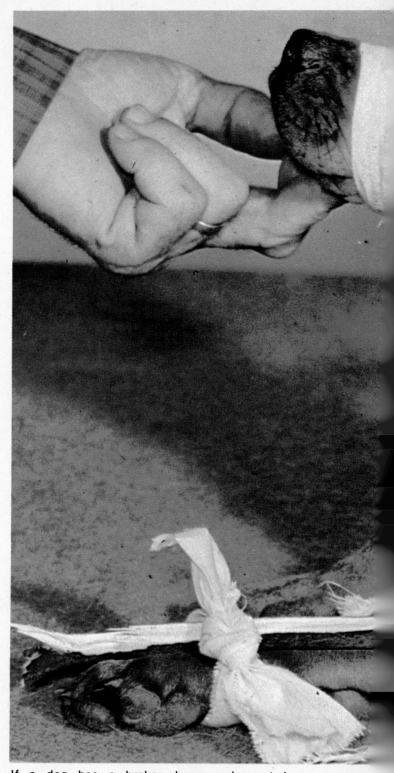

If a dog has a broken bone and must be transported, tie the mouth to ensure that the animal will not bite while in pain. A straight stick then may be applied as a splint and will serve to keep the bone from moving while the dog is in transit. If possible, carry the animal in a blanket.

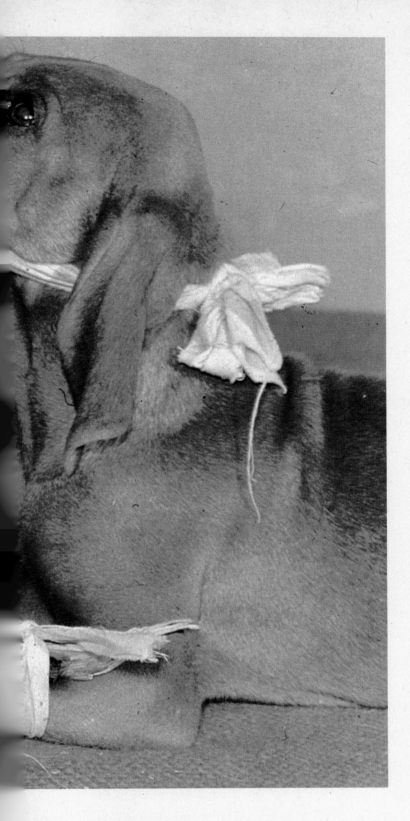

Alkalis

The most common one is drain cleaner. When cleaning drains some of the caustic may be left over and be thrown into the garbage. It takes but a few crystals to cause damage. *Symptoms:* Intense salivation, often followed by nausea, vomiting and expression of pain. *Treatment:* Neutralize the caustic by giving vinegar or lemon juice.

Garbage poisoning

Partially decomposed food in which certain food poisoning organisms have developed can be deadly, but usually there is time to save the dog. *Symptoms:* Trembling is usually the first sign, followed by prostration. When botulism posioning is the cause, the dog becomes limp all over as if he lacked strength in his muscles, especially the neck. Frequently the dog is unable to vomit voluntarily. *Treatment:* Empty the stomach, using peroxide, and when the nausea has ended give Epsom salts or some other quick-acting laxative.

Cyanide

Many cyanide poisonings are malicious, but not all. Because so many surburbanites are troubled by ground moles, thousands of packages of mole poisons are sold annually. The property owner buries them in mole burrows and the cyanide in them kills the moles. Unfortunately, curious dogs see or smell the place where the ground has been freshly dug, scratch up the mole poison and eat it. Many mole poisons contain cyanide, but not enough to produce a fatal effect. *Symptoms:* If you think your dog has swallowed some, take a sniff of his breath and the odor of almond will be quite clear. Look at his gums and tongue, which will be blue. He will show pain and have trouble breathing. *Treatment:* Give peroxide (50-50 with water). You may save him. But let your veterinarian carry on from there.

Warfarin

This most common of all rat poisons, fortunately for dog owners, must be eaten for three or four meals to actually cause death. Death is caused by internal bleeding. Even two meals will cause some ill effects. *Symptoms:* Paleness of the gums, lips and tongue. General overall weakness. *Treatment:* In the early stages, keeping the dog away from warfarin will enable him to recover. In the last stages no treatment is known. Transfusions have been given, but they produce only temporary improvement. Consult your veterinarian. In time an antidote or effective treatment may be discovered.

Phosphorus

This is another common rodent poison. Its effects on dogs are cruel. *Symptoms:* Often causes writhing pain. The breath always has a garlic odor; diarrhea begins quite rapidly. The dog first becomes prostrated, then goes into a coma and dies. *Treatment:* Phosphorus circulating in the bloodstream damages internal organs. The quickest possible treatment is essential. Peroxide, which also causes vomiting, is the antidote. Even though you save your dog's life it may be a long time before he acts like his old self.

Thallium

This is one of the commonest insect and rodent poisons in use today. It is a slow poison, symptoms of which sometimes develop days after ingestion, at which time only supportive veterinary treatment is effective. *Symptoms:* When large amounts have been ingested, salivating and drooling, nausea and vomiting, diarrhea and expressions of pain appear. *Treatment:* Table salt given as quickly as possible after ingestion of the poison.

Paint

This covers a broad term. What actually poisons are the pigments used in its composition, and the lead in the white lead which gives paint substance and adhesive properties. Paris green is commonly used as a pigment. This is an arsenical, and any dog that has licked fresh green paint should be considered a possible poisoning suspect and be properly treated. The lead in the paint (if it is a lead-base paint) complicates the problem. *Symptoms:* Tell-tale paint around the dog's face and lips or fresh paint on the body should make one suspicious, especially when he exhibits pain in the abdomen, perhaps trembles, breathes rapidly and constantly moves about until he becomes prostrated.

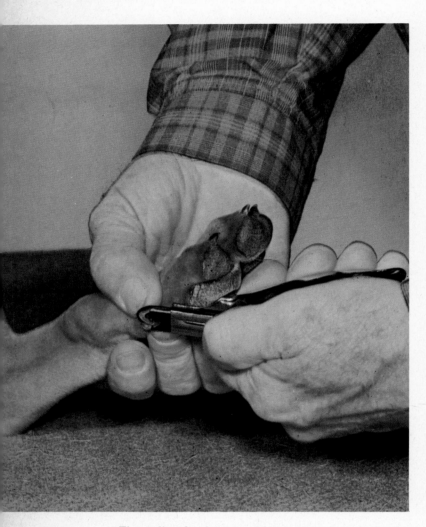

The nails of a dog should be trimmed periodically to prevent scratching. If a dog has an injury in the forequarters or around the head, a natural inclination is to scratch with a hind foot. This can cause irritation and infection, so it is best to keep the nails short and let the wound heal without interference.

Treatment: Empty the stomach, and after the nausea has subsided give a teaspoonful of Epsom salts in water. The lead part is the least dangerous, but the arsenic from the Paris green may, if much has been absorbed from the paint, mean a protracted period of convalescence.

Strychnine

Those who use strychnine to poison foxes or other varmints frequently poison dogs too. Like cyanide, strychnine poisoning can be malicious. *Symptoms:* The typical violent twitching and trembling between short periods of quiet can never be forgotten by anyone who has seen a dog with strychnine poisoning. These tremblings usually end in death, the duration of suffering being dependent on how much poison was consumed. *Treatment:* If you can take your dog to the veterinarian alive, the chances are that he can save him. He will inject a drug which will counteract the trembling and empty the stomach, usually in that order.

If you happen to have some sleeping capsules—one of the barbiturates (1 ½ gr.) such as phenobarbital, nembutal or seconal—etc., empty the contents of four or five (if your dog weighs about forty pounds) into a little water, dissolve it and give by the lip pocket method. Then hurry to the veterinarian, or if he is near enough ask him to come to you.

Copper

Copper is occasionally eaten in the form of copper sulphate. Dogs have chewed corroded areas over copper pipes and been made sick, but the ingredients in spray materials most commonly cause poisoning. *Symptoms:* Expressions of pain, sometimes convulsions, twitching and, if enough time has elapsed, the dog may void blue-colored stools. *Treatment:* Use peroxide to induce vomiting, provided you can treat the pet soon after he has eaten the copper. Better, let your veterinarian treat him.

Plant sprays

These consist of a wide variety of drugs, with new ones coming on the market every year. For some there are no antidotes. The old culprits were mostly arsenicals and copper, discussed above.

Immediate first aid is needed for a dog that has been struck by a car. The police, the local veterinarian, and the owner of the dog should be notified, and the dog should be kept warm and calm while awaiting professional help.

Insect sprays

For DDT there is no published antidote.

Chlordane

Chlordane is sprinkled on lawns or gardens to kill grubs and thus eliminate ground moles that live on grubs, or around the base of homes to eradicate termites, and is an ever present danger for pets. It is a slower poison than some. If you can't get to a veterinarian quickly, induce vomiting immediately.

Sodium fluoride

This is sprinkled on floors and the lower shelves of closets to destroy roaches and ants. Dogs often drop bones or meat on it, then eat the meat and are poisoned. Induce immediate vomiting; then get to vet.

"Ant Cups" or "Buttons"

These have long been a favorite means of ridding premises of these annoying insect pests. Ant cups are metal bottle caps filled with sweetened, poisoned material. Dogs often chew them, sometimes swallowing the top along with the poison. They are made with thallium or arsenic, so read the contents label on the package and follow the directions in treating with the proper antidote.

Fortunately most of these pest poisons are being replaced with safer materials.

Radiator antifreeze

This is often ethylene glycol. It may drip from a leak and, since it tastes sweet, dogs are tempted to lap it up. This substance changes to oxylic acid which does the real poisoning. *Symptoms:* Chiefly pain and nausea. *Treatment:* If you are sure the dog has lapped antifreeze, empty his stomach and give a teaspoonful of bicarbonate of soda dissolved in water; then consult your veterinarian.

Chocolate

The theobromine in black cooking chocolate, similar to caffeine in coffee, is very concentrated. Many dogs have stolen and eaten bars of this which, while it may not have killed them, have produced such symptoms of shaking that their actions were frightening. *Treatment:* Empty the stomach by using peroxide and if you have any bar-

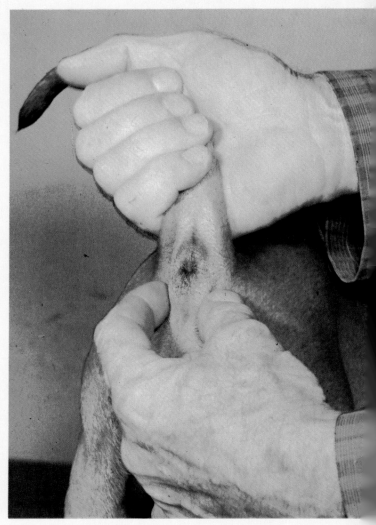

Firmly grasp the tail of a dog and check the anal glands, which can become impacted if not kept clean. If a dog has difficulty eliminating, the animal gets uncomfortable and then will decide not to eat. At the same time, an abscess can form in the rectum, causing greater complications that can be very painful.

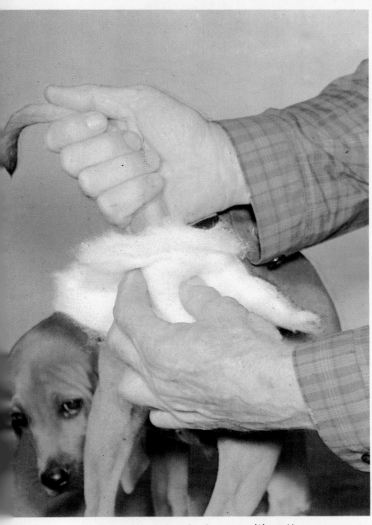

Softly wiping the dog's rear with cotton eases any discomfort and cleanses the anal glands. Sometimes there is intestinal obstruction, such as splintered bones that the dog ate, which causes blockage in the rectum.

biturate sleeping pills dissolve some in an ounce of water. Don't exceed a 1 ½ grain capsule for each ten pounds of the dog's weight. Give by the lip pocket method. Then let your veterinarian carry on. He may inject a sedative intravenously and quickly counteract the nervous symptoms. Be sure to tell him what medication you have given by mouth.

Laurel and rhododendron leaves

It is surprising how often dogs have been poisoned by these plants. No one has been able to discover the attraction. *Symptoms:* Nausea soon develops. There is profuse salivation and a general weakness. *Treatment:* Even if you know the dog has vomited, produce more with peroxide. Follow with Epsom salts for a physic.

Sleeping pills

It may surprise you to know that many dogs somehow manage to find and eat sleeping pills. They must swallow them whole or the bitterness would cause the drug to be rejected. The fact that this kind of poisoning is fairly frequent makes one wonder whether the pills are not given to the dog purposely, perhaps by neighbors who put them in food to cause the dog's owner to keep his pet at home but give lethal overdoses by accident. *Symptoms:* Should your dog come home and go into a deep sleep, suspect barbiturate poisoning. *Treatment:* Before he is too deeply unconscious to be able to swallow, empty his stomach with peroxide and give him half a cup of strong coffee. Then take him to the veterinarian.

BREEDING ACCIDENTS

A question commonly asked of many veterinarians is what to do when a pair of dogs is found sexually united where the sight is causing embarrassment. How to separate them? Policemen should know, but few do, and they are among those who telephone an expert for information.

All kinds of methods have been tried, from throwing water on them to the use of kind words.

This is a natural phenomenon which unfortunately can give children incorrect ideas about sex. Dogs remain united from fifteen to forty-five minutes. Think what would happen to a pair of breeding wolves if they could not separate quickly when danger approached! A fight will cause the dog's penis to shrink quickly, so frighten him—the bitch does not control the tying.

If you can find something to make a loud noise use it. You may find a pair of dogs in the street. The slamming of a board on the sidewalk will make a frightening sound. Or pound on a metal pan with a heavy spoon or stick.

If the male is small enough, another way to frighten him is to hold him up off the ground and shake him furiously.

Accidental breeding

Every year thousands of bitches are bred accidentally. While in heat almost any bitch will endeavor to escape, and males will perform unusual feats to get into their quarters to breed them.

Suppose your bitch was bred and you do not want her puppies or the trouble of raising them to the age when you can place them. What should you do? An enema seldom has any effect.

If you have her spayed, this is permanent; and if you wish later that she could have puppies, you may regret your action.

Your veterinarian can inject a drug into the bitch and give you tablets for her if you contact him within twenty-four hours of the breeding. This will prolong her present period of heat but will not prevent future litters.

The birth of puppies

Veterinarians will tell you that many of their clients believe that this natural function requires first aid. In the vast majority of cases all that is needed is common sense. Books have been published which give us distorted ideas about the phenomenon. Some insist that you must use disinfected scissors and cut each umbilical cord an inch from the abdomen. One even suggests that you tie it with sterile thread. Each afterbirth must be burned, etc. etc., and other unnecessary procedures are advised.

The best aid is to be prepared. Give the bitch a place where she can whelp undisturbed. She will clean the puppies, lick-

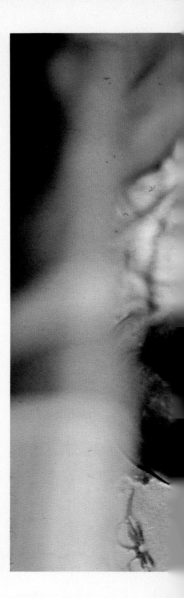

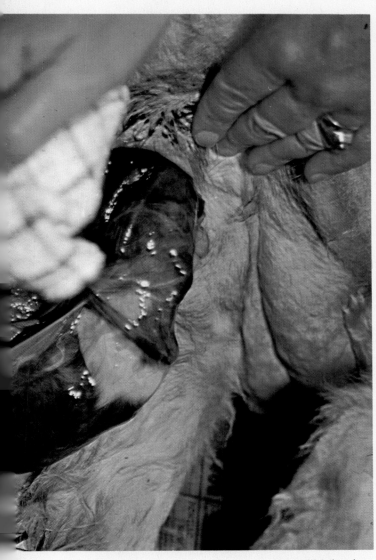

Usually a dam will bring her whelps into the world totally unassisted, but sometimes problems can ocur; in such cases, immediate action is necessary. Each pup is inside a placental sac, and that sac must be removed at birth so that the pup may breathe. If not removed by the dam herself, the breeder must do this by opening the membrane around the face and stimulating circulation in the pup.

ing off any fetal membranes which may cling to them. She will chew off the cord and eat the afterbirth, leaving her nest as clean as possible of all but fluids which escape.

Some people fill her whelping bed with old cloths. These frequently become mixed up with the puppies and the mother accidentally smothers them. If you live where you can buy soft straw or hay, make a bed for her in the shape of a large saucer. The pups will roll into a pile at the bottom of it. Left to herself that is the kind of nest she would make.

If you live in the city, put several thicknesses of absorbent cloth on the floor of the whelping box and tack it down so it will remain flat. Change it after whelping is over.

Sometimes first aid is called for during whelping. If you find a puppy partly outside of the vulva, and the mother's straining can't move it any farther, place a piece of cloth over it and gently pull it out. A splash of fluid will follow, so be prepared. Don't wait until the puppy is dead and gangrenous. Be prompt and you may save its life.

Should the bitch strain but after several hours accomplish nothing, it may signal the need for a Caesarian operation. Ask your veterinarian. There should be no delay if living puppies are to be born or removed surgically.

HUNTING AND FISHING WOUNDS

Many a rabbit hunter has missed the rabbit and shot his dog. The dog will usually scream in pain and will frequently run for some distance. He may be difficult to find. When he has been found he may be in shock, the severity of which depends on the number of pellets and the force behind them. He may even appear dead and will have to be revived by artificial respiration.

Do not try to remove the shots. That's a job for a veterinarian who will X-ray him and take out all he can find, especially those in dangerous locations, such as joints, where they can cause lameness. Some of the pellets will be lodged against bones; others may may be loose in muscles where they can cause pain with every movement. If the veterinarian does not find them all on the first visit, further X-rays may bring them to light and they can then be removed. Sometimes a small cluster of pellets will be seen in one location. After removal of the mass, however, one may still remain.

Large single bullet wounds are another matter. Even a .22 caliber can snap a leg bone or even shatter it. This calls for application of a splint and a hurried trip to the animal hospital. Jaws, shoulder blades, and backs are often broken. This does not mean the dog must be destroyed, not by any means. The bullet may be extracted, fractures set and, if the spinal cord was not damaged or severed by the shot, the small chips of bone may be removed by the veterinarian. In time your dog may be as good as new.

Fish hooks

A fisherman casting with a new rod may attach a lure that attracts his dog and catch him instead of a fish! Or perhaps the dog snatches at an old worm left on a fish hook. Even lures with no bait have been bitten by dogs. Veterinarians will tell you that these are common occurrences.

Since most fishermen have cutting pliers as part of their equipment, it is strange how helpless they are at relieving their dogs of the pain caused by a fishhook through the lip.

It is only necessary to apply a mouth tie to the dog and cut the hook in the middle, taking half out from each side of the lip. If the hook is embedded in the lip, that is a job for the veterinarian who will use a general or local anesthetic and push the point through the lip and then cut the hook into two pieces. Dogs have chewed lures with three sets of hooks, most of which have sunk into the tongue and lips. If your dog does that, don't try first aid unless a vet is not available. If you have to, cut the hooks to get the body of the lure out of his mouth, and when you can get him to the veterinarian let that expert remove the points of the hooks from their deep positions.

Traps

Dogs occasionally come home dragging small animal traps tightly on their feet.

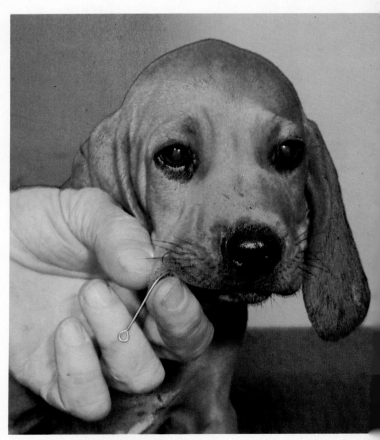

If a dog should get a fishhook caught in the lip, the hook should be cut in the middle so that half can be taken out from each side of the lip. This can be done with a cutting pliers (below), and the dog must be held firmly.

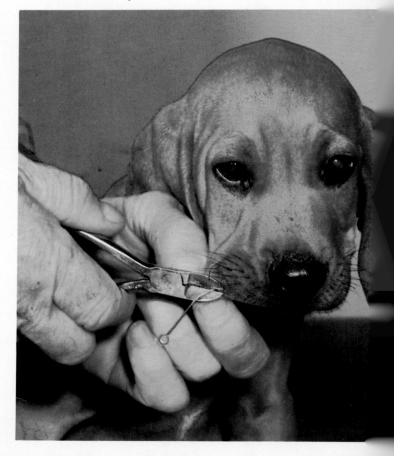

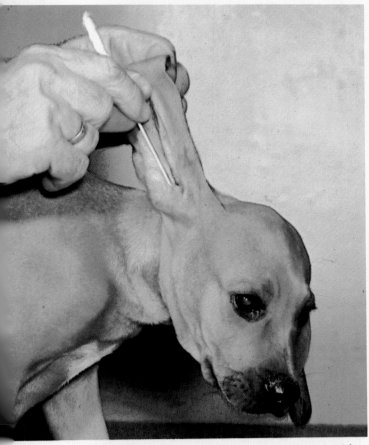

Ears are delicate inside and should be checked for wax, mites, and secretion. When ear troubles bother a dog, the animal will shake its head and rub its ears along a wall or on a floor as a signal for help. To prevent irritation, keep the ears clean.

Sometimes, however, they become trapped in a large fox or wolf trap and cannot free the trap to drag it home.

Before attempting to remove a trap, remember the dog is usually in great pain. Therefore, protect yourself accordingly. Hold the dog's leg so the trap is on the ground. Put one foot on the spring on one side, the other foot on the other spring and press down. The tension on the jaws will relax and they will open. Then gently pull the dog's leg upward and out of the trap.

Some smaller traps have a spring on only one side, making them easier to open.

Examine the dog's foot for trap damage. Sometimes small muskrat traps will not cut the skin though larger traps may severe skin and tendons. When that happens the repair is up to your veterinarian.

Porcupine quills

If you live in areas where there are porcupines, don't take your dog into the woods from late afternoon on through the night without having a pair of pliers in your pocket to pull quills should your dog attack one of these spiny creatures. He may get a mouthful of long white quills, but usually his shoulder and forelegs are also covered with short black quills where the porcupine has slapped him with his heavy tail. This is his defense mechanism and the tail quills are much harder to pull than are the larger ones from the back.

Here is a case of first aid *par excellence*. You may have no time to rush the dog to a veterinarian. If you have pliers, do the next best thing—pull quills. Later the veterinarian will anesthetize your dog who by then might well be in a state of shock.

Tie your dog to a tree with his leash so he can't run away. Put a stick in his mouth so you can examine the inside of the mouth, the tongue and throat. Pull every quill. If some are sticking into the lips, push them through and pull them out on the other side. Freeing the mouth of quills makes him feel easier and he will not frantically fight with his paws.

Next, remove quills from around the dog's eyes, over the joints and in the chest. Now pull all the quills from the rest of the body.

If one breaks off, you can't stop to excavate it because the quills will be moving inward with every movement of the dog's muscles. Those which go inside the shoulder muscles will usually work upward, and during the next few days you will feel their sharp points protruding from the back just above the shoulders (the withers).

The quills in the front of the body will usually do little damage beyond causing temporary lameness until they have worked out, but those penetrating the area over the ribs, or the body behind the ribs, can cause death and should be the first to be pulled.

Examine the head carefully to assure yourself that no quills are pointing towards the eyes.

Next day and for several days feel your dog all over for points of quills and pull them out. You may wonder why the dog doesn't die of tetanus, but porcupine quills, as dirty as they are, rarely cause lockjaw.

What I have said may sound simpler than it really is. If your dog is a big one, heroic measures and all your strength and patience may be called for just to control him. Your leg wrapped about his body could help to restrain him.

BLOAT

Unless you own a Great Dane, St. Bernard, Newfoundland or other large breed of dog you may never know the danger of bloat. But all giant breed owners have been told of the danger. Usually about five to six hours after a meal, gas develops in the stomach and causes the abdominal cavity to swell to huge proportions. On tapping the side, it sounds hollow and drum-like. The ballooning continues until pressure on the lungs and heart becomes intense. In severe cases the dog may die unless the pressure is quickly relieved.

If you can hustle your dog to a veterinarian in time, he will be able to help. If it is too late, the dog, although relieved, may face a lingering death.

In the early stages it is sometimes possible to gently squeeze, prod and knead the abdomen which may produce great volumes of gas to be expelled by belching. Only if no help is available should one try an ab-

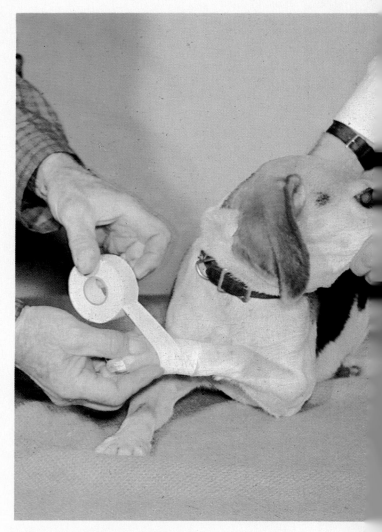

Adhesive tape keeps a bandage in place and also shields the bandage, as well as the wound, from dirt and infection. It also protects the wound from being bumped inadvertently.

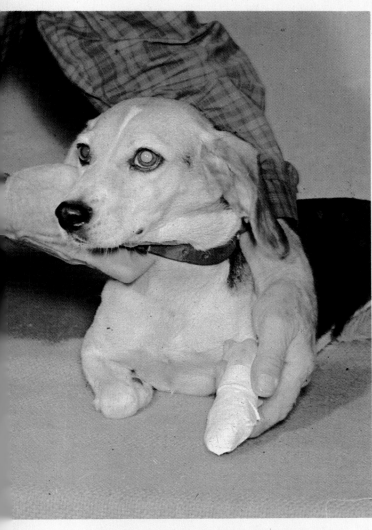

When an entire paw is bandaged and wrapped with adhesive tape, the dog tends to hide the other paw and protect it! The animal knows that care must be taken and that healing does not just happen overnight.

dominal tap with a hollow needle. Such a needle may be improvised by cutting off about four inches of the rib of an umbrella, sharpening it and plunging it through the skin and stomach wall to allow the gas to escape. If you are lucky you may be happily surprised to find that you have saved the dog.

For a stimulant, strong coffee may work wonders. A teaspoonful of instant coffee in a half cup of warm water, given to the dog by the lip pocket method, is enough for a fairly large one; two teaspoonfuls for a Great Dane or other giant dog. This, of course, is given after the gas has been let out of the stomach.

It is imperative for a veterinarian to see such a case for many reasons, not the least of which is to determine whether the stomach has rotated out of position. If it has, surgery may be the only method of correction.

SNAKE BITES

There is very little one can do in the way of first aid for a dog bitten by a poisonous snake, unless the bite is on a foot or low down on the leg.

Treatment: Apply a tourniquet to try to keep the poison from spreading upwards. Release the tourniquet for 30 seconds every ten minutes and reapply. Hurry him to a veterinarian. Usually snake bites occur too far from any help. Some vets advise cutting an "X" deeply at the site of the bite in the hope that bleeding will partly wash out the venom. A sharp knife is necessary and, needless to say, the dog should be very securely tied, both to keep his mouth closed and to prevent him from running away. Suction to the lanced area could help.

SKUNK SPRAYING

No one wants to keep a dog that has been sprayed by a skunk about his premises, waiting for the odor to disappear, though it will in time and more quickly in hot weather.

If your dog is sprayed, wash him with detergent and after rinsing, rub canned tomato juice into the coat, allowing it to soak in for ten minutes; then rebathe him with detergent and rinse. Repeat each step until the odor is gone. The amount of juice is determined by the dog's size and the thoroughness with which the skunk anointed the dog.

The dog may damage his eyes by rubbing them to rid himself of the odor and because the chemical irritates. However, it causes only a local irritation—never blindness.

THUNDERSTORMS

Many dogs actually suffer in thunderstorms. They let us know when one is approaching before we are conscious of it, thus allowing us time to give a sedative or tranquillizer previously obtained from the veterinarian.

Some dogs are less distressed when close to a loved one.

The cellar or an inside room may help such a sensitive pet, and playing the radio with loud volume often helps overshadow the thunder.

FREEZING AND FROSTBITE

With any reasonable amount of acclimation, dogs can withstand long periods of frigid temperature, even running ten miles across ice at 0°F. with no ill effects.

Most problems of exposure arise after a dog has been injured, entangled in briers or caught on a wire fence by his collar. Even if his body is stiff, if the heart is beating bring him into room temperature and raise his temperature slowly, depending on massage rather than artificial heating devices. This is one of the few times when whisky may be of help as an initial stimulant. Later, when the blood is flowing and pain may be present, it acts as a depressant. One tablespoonful with one tablespoonful of water and one tablespoonful of sugar should be given at thirty minute intervals for a thirty-pound dog.

True frostbite is slow to heal and your veterinarian should handle the problem. Antibiotics are often given after freezing and frostbite to prevent exposure problems such as pneumonia.

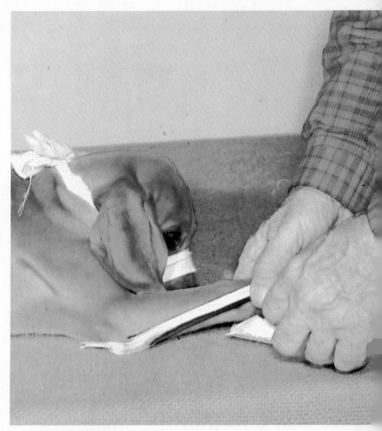

To a certain extent, a dog is dependent upon people and places trust in people. The animal appreciates care and understanding, especially when hurt.

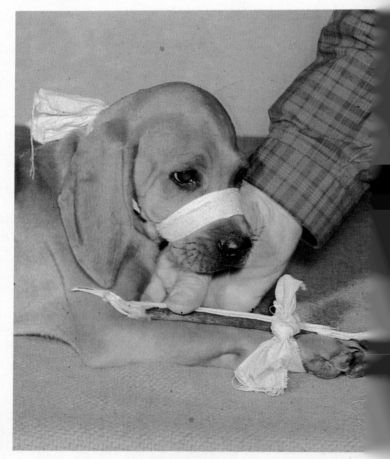

Special attention to a dog that is sick is returned a hundredfold in devotion.

SOME SIMPLE FIRST AID "DON'TS"

Don't try to treat serious problems without a veterinarian's advice.

Don't heed the well-meant advice of the untrained, self-named expert.

Don't put hot compresses on a recent injury.

Don't put cold compresses on an old injury.

Don't leave a tourniquet in place for more than thirty minutes without releasing it for thirty seconds.

Don't put a bandage on an extremity too tightly unless the bandage is only temporary.

Don't overdose with home remedies such as aspirin.

Don't use human remedies on your dog without a veterinarian's advice.

Don't leave needles and pins and other lethal objects where a dog can reach them.

Don't permit your dog the luxury of running loose unattended; garbage, poisons and automobiles are waiting to maim or kill him.

Don't leash a dog where he can jump over a barrier and hang himself.

Don't leave a dog in a motor vehicle in the sun with the windows closed; in the heat of summer don't leave him in the car at all.

Don't use whisky for all your dog's ills—it's an initial stimulant, then a depressant.

Don't try to be your own veterinarian.

Children should be taught to respect a dog and not to mistreat the animal. Such caring youngsters can be excellent nurses who speed the recovery of a sick dog.

Index

(Page numbers in parentheses refer
to illustrations.)